# STRANGE ENCOUNTERS

# STRANGE ENCOUNTERS

## John Toohey

PRESS

# VULPINE

## PRESS

Published by Vulpine Press in the United Kingdom in 2024

ISBN: 978-1-83919-589-1

www.vulpine-press.com

For Edda, who considers adventure a duty

# CONTENTS

# INTRODUCTION

Explorers' reports of their expeditions into the unknown usually make tedious reading. Weeks pass without any change in the scenery but they trudge on, diligently entering readings of latitude and longitude every morning and evening, along with lifeless descriptions of the topography and the weather, while taking whole days to cover distances that back home were as far as the nearest bus stop.

Back home they were attached to colleges as surveyors and geologists, and in the military they were engineers. The office not the jungle or the desert was their natural environment and they could be brilliant at observation and analysis, but it was a bonus if they had any literary flourish.

That's why the best accounts are by people who never intended to go out there. Once they landed, in a place they never wanted to be, feelings rather than facts were all that mattered.

There were numerous new opportunities for death and the only way to suffocate fear was to embrace resignation. They didn't have the vocabulary to describe what they saw so everything they wrote or said was a misinterpretation. The inhabitants were not living on land they intended to covet so they were objects of curiosity. What these people left behind had a nuance in opposition to the official story. It was seldom first-hand, and it wasn't always words but it had an unambiguous presence.

1

"This is my story, or what remains of it. Make of it what you will."

Let's begin with three stories about people who went out into the unknown, even if only in their own heads.

In 1952 labourers in Yangzhou were demolishing part of the old city walls to use the stones for roadworks when they uncovered a western style headstone with an inscription in Latin. It read in part, "Here lies Caterina, daughter of the deceased lord Domenico de Vilioni, who died in A.D. 1342, in the month of June." The headstone featured cherubs lifting a child from a tomb and a figure being executed, which could be a reference to the martyr Saint Catherine of Alexandria, beheaded about 305CE, though that figure and her executioner appear to be distinctly Chinese.

A few years later another headstone, memorializing her brother Antonio, was also discovered close by. He had died in 1344. We know nothing more about the two, though a little about their father, who came from a line of merchants who traded in Asia, and even the surname is disputed, but there's general agreement that both were children. The journey from Italy to China involved a sea voyage to Constantinople or Jerusalem, either way far less treacherous than the route across Europe, and then overland through deserts and mountain ranges, into the vestiges of the Mongol empire, which was already being carved up among warlords. It could take four or five years, and it's hard to believe very young children could have survived the overland crossing along the Silk Road, or that their father was willing to risk taking them along it, so unless they were old enough, about ten when they left Genoa, they had to be born in China. That being so, they spoke a dialect of Mandarin in public and when their father talked of Venice or Genoa as home, to the children these were distant and mysterious lands, their Xanadu.

Marco Polo had left China about fifty years earlier, and before him his father Niccolò and uncle Maffeo had already travelled the well beaten path between Europe and China, following William of Rubruck, Nicholas Ascelin, Giovanni del Carpini, John of Montecorvino, various Nestorian heretics, Roman emissaries and just possibly a team of Greek acrobats – and all these were travelling east. How many came the other way isn't a fair question since the Mongols had invaded Europe into Croatia, and the Three Wise Men in Matthew's Gospel came "from the East", which could mean anywhere from Christian Byzantium to pagan Peking.

Not long after arriving back in Venice, Marco Polo suffered a small misfortune that turned out to be a stroke of luck. Venice was at war with Genoa (one of those repetitious conflicts between city states that drove Italian history until the Risorgimento in 1871) and Polo was captured and imprisoned; not in a cold, damp cell, more a well catered apartment and, this was the real hidden blessing, he had to share it with Rustichello da Pisa, a liar, hustler and fraud or, in medieval terms, a novelist.

He urged Polo to put their incarceration to good use and dictate his account of his travels. Called at various times *Il Milione, The Book of Marvels of the World,* or *Marco Polo's Travels,* it became a bestseller, though that phrase sounds jarring for a manuscript produced before Gutenberg's printing press, and when most of the population was functionally illiterate. It

3

was at least translated into several languages and widely read by (or to) merchants and bankers who knew China had money but couldn't work out how to get their hands on it.

Historians and literary analysts have wondered ever since which words belonged to Rustichello and which were Polo's. In 1995, Frances Wood proposed that all of the *Travels* was invented, her argument resting on what both men missed: tea, the Great Wall, chopsticks and other details the most careless traveller would have noted. But in filtering Polo's words, Rustichello was in no hurry to get to the facts. The people of Sumatra "eat human flesh, and all other sorts of flesh" and "worship a variety of objects, for each man adores throughout the day the first thing he sees when he rises in the morning". There's a lot of cannibalism in the *Travels*, and other strange customs, and displays of great wealth, because Rustichello knew what held readers' attentions, and it wasn't always descriptions of cutlery or dinner etiquette.

It was Rustichello, not Marco Polo, who made *The Travels* a bestseller, and in the process, he articulated a law that has never quite left us. Without literary talent, the explorer or adventurer must have an amanuensis, able to take otherwise tiresome, bloated descriptions and transform them into taut narratives. If explorers' journals belong in their own literary genre, and according to some major publishing houses they do, then there is no sub-genre less thrilling than the badly written explorer's journal.

Here is a single sentence from Ensign Robert Dale's 1829 journal of the exploration of the Helena River outside of Perth, Western Australia. He is crossing the sand bars at Heirisson

Island, just east of what is now the city centre, and heading into what will become Rivervale, a semi-industrial suburb, but in 1829 Dale and his party were the first Europeans to set foot in it.

At a quarter before 8 o'clock, a.m. left Perth, and forded the Swan River at the islands; at 9 proceeded in an E. direction over a sandy and thickly wooded country, and in five miles crossed a swamp lying E. and W., and soon afterwards a rather extensive one to the S.E., which we again crossed to the S.W.; two miles and a half further passed a small one lying S.E. and N.W.; we continued our walk about the same distance of two miles and a half when we came to the dry bed of a stream, and continued along its banks till we reached the mountains, where we bivouaced at 4 p.m. in a small valley with pretty good soil, and grass in it, but having a rocky surface.

It was early December. A shame he didn't set out about six weeks earlier because he would have caught the wildflowers in bloom, and perhaps been inspired to write a rapturous description of nature at its strangest, most fertile and vivid, except if the above passage is any guide, the only detail he cared about was the soil quality.

Twenty-eight years earlier, a crew from the Baudin Expedition mapping the West Australian coast had rowed up the Swan River from its mouth near present day Fremantle. They were led by François-Antoine Heirisson, who the island in the middle of the Swan is named after. The Baudin Expedition was charged with mapping and sounding, and also collecting botanical and animal specimens, and under strict instructions not to antagonize the human inhabitants. Charles Bailly, a mineralogist, sat in

5

the boat with Heirisson, noting the shore with a sharp eye for changes in rock colouring and texture. Unlike Dale, he understood those changes in the geology were significant, though precise explanations still eluded him. In the afternoon, the crew reached the sand bars.

> All at once we heard a terrible noise that filled us with terror; it was something like the roaring of a bull, but much louder, and seemed to come from the reeds close to us. At this formidable sound we lost all desire to go ashore, and though benumbed with cold we preferred to pass the night on the water.

Not much there in the word count, but it is riven with the vulnerability that men who have entered a strange new world must feel.

Rustichello knew something that Dale didn't, but which Bailly also understood innately. Whatever other skills and talents the explorer possessed, storytelling was the most important.

The first question asked of the explorer on his or her return was "what did you see out there?" If the answer was, "good soil here, bad there," the explorer had fulfilled one requirement while consigning respect and reputation to the dustbin of history. Posterity demanded humanity, and no surprises that despite being the first European to explore the interior of Western Australia, Dale remains a minor figure; a shame he didn't pull off a Burke and Wills, set out with intentions to cross the continent, prove utterly incompetent and perish in the desert. He would have at least got a statue.

The narration of *The Travels* constantly flips between Polo's first person and Rustichello's third. That shifting voice gives the narrative an objective distance, so even stories that sound fantastic can never be entirely dismissed. Rustichello is only reporting what Marco Polo told him, while Marco Polo is merely repeating what others have said. Neither man can fairly be accused of lying.

But despite the literary flourishes of *The Travels*, there's the feeling that for the outsider's view of Yuan China there were two other, more reliable and authentic voices, although they've only left for us their headstones.

Caterina and Antonio saw China through the singular gaze of being outsiders with no experience of any other world. Their silence is a reminder that for all its bombast and filigree, Marco Polo's account lacks their credibility.

*

In the Spring of 1503 a French trader, Binot Paulmier de Gonneville, set out from Le Havre for the Spice Islands, as the Indonesian Moluccas were known. This was about fifteen years before the Magellan Expedition circumnavigated the globe (though not Magellan himself; he was killed in the Philippines) and most of the map of the world was still guesswork. A storm swept in off the southern coast of Africa and de Gonneville's ship was blown off course.

After drifting terrified and aimlessly for some time, the ship ended up on a coast somewhere in the unknown southern half. Fortunately, the land was inhabited and for six months de Gonneville and his crew lived happily among the natives.

The people seemed to have worked something out: their lives followed simple but harmonious routines: fishing, making things, cooking. Economics, philosophy, religion: all the damage western civilizations inflicted upon themselves were absent, but the people were also curious. Once the crew had mended the ship, they were preparing to depart for home when a chieftain's son named Essoméric asked to join them. By now de Gonneville knew enough of the local language and Essoméric enough of French to not only get along but for both to think the idea was thoroughly splendid. So he boarded and some weeks or months later the *L'Espoir* limped back into le Havre, the crew exhausted but relieved. Ordinary sailors in the 1500s never really liked travelling too far from home.

Not so Essoméric. Apparently, he took to Renaissance France, with its interminable wars and frequent outbreaks of religious heresies, like a duck to water. He married and raised a family, and soon, just like any average French citizen of the age, he disappeared from the record books.

We only know of his existence because in 1654 a descendant and scholarly monk, Abbé Jean Paulmier, wrote to Pope Alexander VII advocating for an expedition to Essoméric's homeland, which he believed had to be the fabled Terra Australis. The Pope was encouraging, and even drew up a scheme to install a bishopric on the new land, but for various reasons the plan fell through. What survived was a renewed vigour in the search for Terra Australis that lasted one hundred and fifty years.

It turned up on maps, complete with named geographical features like rivers and mountain ranges, and sometimes towns, with inhabitants, who were generally semi-naked and lived in grass huts, because anything more sophisticated was an implied threat. For playwrights and novelists on the other hand it was a tabula rasa, devoid of any features so they were free to add their own, which essentially meant their personal utopias: a land where the problems of economics, religion and philosophy had been solved with elegant simplicity.

"These Memoirs were thought so curious, that they were kept *Secret* in the Closet of a late Great *Minister of State,* and never Published till now since his Death." So began a 1676 work of fiction with a very long title that can be truncated to *A New Discovery OF Terra Incognita Australis, or the Southern World, by James Sadeur, a French-man.*

The author was Gabriel de Foigny and very little of his life has survived on public record, but the detail that he was a defrocked monk, kicked out of the Church for sexual misconduct, is unsurprising given his ideas on gender and religion.

> The Australians are hermaphrodites, and if a child is born with only one sex, they kill it as a monster. Their bodies are strong, nimble, and very active, closer in colour to red than to vermilion. They average about eight feet tall. Their faces are moderately long with a broad forehead and bug eyes, a small mouth with lips as red as coral.

Hermaphroditism was a virtue in de Foigny's traumatic world view; we could have been saved from so much suffering if we were all the same gender.

As for religion: *There is no Subject more curious and secret among the* Australians, *than that of their Religion; 'tis a crime of*

*Innovation even to speak of it, either by Dispute or a Form of Explanation.*

Which solved a lot during an era when the Protestant Huguenots were brutally oppressed.

Despite being free to imagine Terra Australis how they wanted, the writers invariably turned in ordinary efforts, precisely because they proposed absurd solutions to complex problems. Merchants and empire builders kept the dream alive with more hard-headed visions, of spices essentially, and gold and silver; anything that would make them rich.

In 1772 Yves-Joseph de Kerguelen-Trémarec believed he had found the fabled land, a cluster of beautifully bleak and desolate volcanic peaks about halfway between South Africa and Western Australia but closer to Antarctica. The absence of any descendants of Essoméric, or even any evidence they had once set foot on the place should have been a warning, but that presupposes Kerguelen wanted to find Terra Australis, when more likely he wanted to be sustained by the dream.

In any case, later travellers who stopped by the Kerguelen Islands did so to break the monotony. There was absolutely no other reason to visit, and no one who had read Paulmier's description of Terra Australis would believe this inhospitable anomaly was the same place.

Throughout this period however there was never any doubt regarding Paulmier, or his ancestor. Both were useful during an era of colonial assertions. Read one way, Paulmier could be claiming his ancestor reached Brazil, before the Portuguese, another and France could insist it had entitlement to the South Pacific.

What no one ever did was trace back through the records for hard evidence of Essoméric, or de Gonneville. When later historians tried they found (just as they suspected) nothing.

De Gonneville and Essoméric were fictions, not fables like de Foigny's utopia. Their creation was an attempt to persuade the authorities to invest in a scheme, and it isn't hard to recognize Paulmier's thinking. As the wars between Catholics and Protestants dragged on in the streets, he had been inspired by reports from de Queirós, Mendaña and other Portuguese and Spanish explorers that there was something out there, and by laying claim to it, obviously, the Church, and France would increase their power. The notion that more than a century later, expeditions would still be leaving French harbours to search for it, or that they'd often sail over the horizon and never be seen again, was no bother to him. Just so long as Pope Alexander signed on to his vision, and quickly.

By the mid-seventeenth century the Dutch had mapped about two thirds including all the west coast of the South Land, but compared to what they'd been told to expect, what they saw was hardly worth reporting back about. Expeditions left Le Havre, searching for a place that didn't exist. A few who used the Dutch charts pushed on and sailed past mangroves for days before landing on long white beaches, but no cities to open trade with, instead a lot of insects, crocodiles, heat, silence. Everything was always disappointment.

The instructions to look for the Great South Land that James Cook was given on his first voyage into the Pacific were a distant echo of Jean Paulmier's scheme. The consequences of those are still felt today.

*

Robert Peary had the face of an arctic explorer; the thousand-mile stare, the result from gazing bleakly into a cold, white sheet for months at a time, and his skin as cracked and beaten as an old leather boxing glove. The face of a man who has seen too much, or, so far as the long arctic winter is concerned, next to nothing.

A lot of people who had dealings with Peary described him as difficult, which is the polite term for thoroughly obnoxious, though even if members of the Peary Arctic Club did, they weren't about to let on. They loved him, or said so in public, and given the club members were some of the wealthiest and most powerful men in New York, there weren't many willing to contradict them, and in 1913 even less so.

Peary had claimed to have reached the North Pole in 1908, which was controversial partly because another man on the expedition, Matthew Henson planted the flag while Peary lay crippled in a tent, and partly because some respectable scientists had looked at the reports, did their calculations and decided neither man got close enough.

Not that ordinary Americans cared about those details. The long, glorious history of exploration had featured men (mostly) who looked outwards, from Europe towards the Pacific, or Africa or Australia. The American version was more inward, being about men (again) who travelled down the Mississippi or crossed the Rockies or headed into the jungles of South America. Peary on the other hand had looked out, and entered one of the last voids, the Arctic, which placed him on the same pedestal as Cook, Magellan, even Columbus.

To the club members Peary was a hero (more so than Henson, who was black, and wouldn't be recognized by the more prestigious Explorers' Club until the 1930s). Now, in 1913, they were putting together a scheme to find a mysterious island called Crocker Land, that Peary had sighted on his failed 1906 expedition to the Pole.

Peary hadn't provided much detail about this Crocker Land. "I seem to see more distinctly the snow-clad summits of a distant land in the northwest above the ice horizon." And though he wanted to climb up its slopes and wondered what new creatures he might find, that and his decision to name the land in honour of one the Peary Arctic Club members, George Crocker, pretty much summed his observations up. It was enough however to inspire the new expedition funded by the American Museum of Natural History and the American Geographical Society.

It was led by geologist Donald Baxter MacMillan. On paper, his credentials were excellent. He had joined Peary's 1908 expedition to the Pole, could navigate, was considered calm under pressure and spent several years conducting ethnographic research on the Inuit and spoke some of the languages. Which makes his actions on the expedition, including the murder of an Inuit guide, really difficult to comprehend. But then, there'd be a lot of unanswered questions about the expedition when MacMillan finally returned, four years later.

The Crocker Land Expedition was the very last to the Arctic in which British and Americans could put faith in their imaginations and wonder what great secrets the white world held. The year before, Robert Falcon Scott and four others in his expedition to the Antarctic had died, weeks after Roald Amundsen beat them to the Pole. The experiences of both teams left no doubt that if there were any secrets worth discovering they wouldn't be surrendered without enormous risk. The Arctic was different. Its fringes were inhabited by the Inuit, and in summer the ice retreated, revealing a greyish tundra washed by the ocean. And something the Americans especially weren't quick to admit: the Russians had been exploring the Arctic since the early seventeenth century. They had mapped the coastline, and if they hadn't tried to reach the pole, it was probably because they knew it was surrounded by ice and there was nothing to gain reaching it.

MacMillan's plan was to take the expedition on the *Diana* to Battle Harbour in Labrador and transfer team and supplies to the *Erik*. Plans would change; they often did on Arctic expeditions, and it was decided the team would meet the *Erik* at St John's instead.

As the *Diana* steamed out of New York on July 2, the Brusilov expedition on the *Svyataya Anna*, which had been looking for a route through the Arctic Sea to the Pacific, was trapped in ice in the Kara Sea, about a third of the way across Russia and below Novaya Zemlya. In a year, fed up with being imprisoned, the navigator, Valerian Albanov, would take thirteen others out to try and walk across the ice to distant Franz Josef Land. With a poor map, only Albanov and one other survived. Nothing has ever been found of Brusilov, the crew who remained with him, or the ship.

Thirteen days out of New York, the *Diana* hit an iceberg. Woken by the collision, MacMillan went into the corridor, in time to see the ship's captain, Waite, hurrying out of his cabin. On a fog strewn night with icebergs drifting close by (this was a year after the *Titanic* struck one), Waite should have been on the bridge through the night. MacMillan wondered, and later, when the *Diana* had limped to a port and been repaired, he thought Waite "seemed to come out of his reverie".

The phrasing is a polite insinuation that Waite was drunk or drugged, and the language matters because until the madness of being trapped in the Arctic took hold, MacMillan was always measured. Peary used superlatives and exclamation marks and wondered what strange phenomena could portend. Macmillan merely reported what the evidence indicated.

So what to make of press reports, published before the *Diana* departed, that he thought there could be a lost race living on Crocker Land?

\*

The explorer stumbles over desert sands, he hacks through jungle vines, he stares helplessly at his broken sextant. No matter the geography, he is essentially the same man, like a G.I. Joe doll with an outfit for every circumstance; ragged, bearded, damp with fever, but driven by a need to see what lies over the next hill or bend in the river. His need is also ours, which is why we recognize the caricature and even find it compulsive. Real or imaginary, we've only asked that he comes back with news of something fabulous; a ruined city, a lost civilization, a vista like something out of a child's image of paradise.

The polar explorers were different. Even when people talked about a northwest passage joining the Atlantic and Pacific oceans, saving the time, risk and expense of sailing around Africa or South America, there was an existential despair that once the ice was reached that was all there would be: ice, brutal cold and a cruel and lonely death. The disastrous Franklin Expedition to the Arctic in 1845 asked that if members of The World's Greatest Empire couldn't survive up there, who could?

All explorers had to be a little mad to expose themselves to such risks as crossing waterless deserts or disease riddled jungles, but polar explorers were in a category on their own. What was the point of reaching the poles if there was nothing of substance to bring back? The only people with anything to gain were the novelists, specifically the people who wrote novels for boys, or grown men who hadn't yet left boyhood. They at least could perpetuate the dream of the sudden encounter with the utterly incredible.

"Lost" races were a thing back at the turn of last century. They weren't lost in any real meaning of the word, merely undiscovered, and to academics like MacMillan their possibility raised sensible, almost prosaic questions about language and culture. These questions were of no use to novelists. From the African jungles to the Himalayas, the Amazon and the Poles, brave men battled their way into strange worlds that defied logic, and history, and common sense. Henry Rider Haggard's Allan Quartermain was in the habit of stumbling upon them. *King Solomon's Mines* and *She* are the best-known examples of a literary genre that took off during the 1880s, that was on its last legs by the start of the First World War, and which has never required a revival.

The most interesting point to lost world stories is that although the writers had complete freedom to imagine their mysterious cultures, they basically stuck to two models. In the first, a society had remained untouched by Western Civilization, prospered and possessed something, usually vast reserves of gold or diamonds but possibly an attitude the explorers wanted, and typically destroyed in their effort to get it. In the other, the explorers found themselves right back at the dawn of time, among dinosaurs and troglodytes, suddenly able to answer the big questions of science, if anyone back home was willing to believe them. These weren't just adventure stories for adolescent men. The lost race was a cry of pain for a vanished past, by people ashamed of the modern world, but even more keenly, for a time when a lot of the world remained unmapped and unclaimed by colonial powers. It was particularly poignant for solidly British writers like Haggard, Conan Doyle and Kipling because now the map of Britain's empire looked complete, decline was inevitable.

The novelists could be lots of things: awful to be around, ranting fascists, but they usually weren't as mad as the people who believed there was sound scientific reasoning behind the idea of lost cultures and new lands.

The idea of a hollow, inhabited Earth goes back at least to classical Greece, and may be much older in cultures without a written language, but it was essentially literary. Writers used it the same way they did Terra Australis, as a dumping ground for philosophical fancies, usually with a knowing wink to the reader that neither of them took its existence seriously. The theory that the interior could be inhabited, and that the likely entrances to this world lay at the poles, was vaguely discussed but didn't catch on until the nineteenth century, when John Symmes and others began pushing it. Symmes's thesis was asinine, but it matters because he laid out the template for the scientific subterranean world as lit, warm, well-watered and stocked with animals. Every advocate after that recycled the imagery. There's a razor's difference between his vision of the underworld and that some evangelical and Pentecostal groups have of the afterlife today.

In 1906 William Reed published *The Phantom of the Poles*, which you could say used science to make the case for the hollow Earth. What it really used was obfuscation and reliance on the reader having only the vaguest knowledge of arctic science to claim that all those anomalies with compasses that explorers reported, the aurora borealis, the midnight sun and other phenomena had one answer.

In Volume I, page 375, of Nansen's "Farthest North," Friday, January 19, 1894, he says: "Splendid wind, with velocity of thirteen to nineteen feet per second; we are going north at a grand rate. The red, glowing twilight is now so bright about midday that if we were in more southern latitudes we should expect to see the sun rise bright and glorious above the horizon in a few minutes; but we shall have to wait a month yet for that." The fact is, Nansen was going into the interior of the earth, while he was under the impression that he was going north.

The leaps in logic, the twisting of Nansen's words, Reed's cunning assuredness that most readers would have to take him at face value, all classic plays from the textbook on how to convince people of the merits of pseudoscience. But none of it would have mattered if there wasn't that desire for a hollow Earth, or an undiscovered race of humans. It articulated a desire for the marvels the world promised when Polo and Paulmier were describing it, a world before it had been explored and mapped and its various societies and natural wonders accounted for. But it was more than just another form of nostalgia for the impossible; what really marked the hollow earthers was their deep and resentful anti-science streak.

Science never denied the existence of anything, but it demanded evidence to support logic, and since that was absent the challenge for hollow earthers was to create a system where evidence wasn't necessary. Christians could do it by giving God powers that rendered evidence meaningless, though after two thousand years of debate there were still fights among believers. The case hollow earthers had to make was even harder. Where Christian fundamentalists could shout "God is real!" hollow earthers could only protest that an underworld was theoretically possible, but how would anyone know unless the Government backed an expedition? As explorers drew closer to the Poles, to the entrance of that imaginable underworld, advocates like Reed felt a sense of urgency.

From what I am able to gather, and from analysis, game of all kinds—tropical and arctic—will be found there; for both warm and cold climates must be in the interior— warm inland and cold near the poles. Sea monsters, and possibly the much-talked-of sea serpent, may also be found, and vast territories of arable land for farming purposes...I also believe that the interior of the earth will be found inhabited. The race or races may be varied, but some at least will be of the Eskimo race, who have found their way in from the exterior. Camping places have been discovered, and relics that did not belong to the present Inuits; nor did the latter know for what purposes certain articles were used.

Now that the image of the explorer is inextricable from colonialism, it's easy to forget that most explorers set out in the name of science, and they tended to return from out there confirming that the world behaved according to laws of nature or physics. MacMillan epitomized that (more than Peary, who liked the glare of publicity). If he had found Crocker Land and met its so far unknown inhabitants, the feeling is the first thing he'd do was collect vocabulary. That wasn't good enough for some people.

MacMillan had ninety years of fatal errors and ignorant decisions to draw on. The worst involved the Inuit, who earlier expeditions had regarded with bafflement and sometimes contempt based on the logic of imperial power. MacMillan understood that any venture into the Arctic required submission to Inuit wisdom.

Boots made of the skin of the forelegs of a polar bear, with a sole of the bearded, or thong, seal, are undeniably the warmest product of the northern Eskimo shoemaker.

At moderately low temperatures, twenty and thirty below, a boot of the forelegs of the caribou is very satisfactory.

The sealskin boot, called the kamik, is the boot in general use among the Eskimos of Smith Sound.

The sole of all the boots is made from the extremely tough skin of the bearded seal {Erignalhus barbatus).

As the expedition prepared to head into the interior and search for Crocker Land, he felt assured that he had accounted for any possible hazard.

*Stretching out before me to the westward there were now nineteen men and fifteen sledges drawn by 165 dogs headed toward that great unknown sector of the Polar Sea, consisting of half a million square miles. The distance from Etah* (the base camp in Greenland) *to the edge of this white spot by air line is 483 statute miles.*

That was January 1914. By May the best laid plans had come apart. The nerves of men whose day jobs involved quiet research in university departments were fraying. Most of the expedition had already returned to Etah, sick with disease and frostbite. One American would stay with MacMillan, Fitzhugh Green, naval ensign with a physics degree, and a man MacMillan increasingly depended on. He sent Green and the Inuit hunter Piugaattoq to the southwest with three days of food. Six days later he still waited for them to return.

Late in the afternoon a black dot appeared on the horizon – something was coming. As the dot approached I could contain myself no longer; the sledge coming must be Pee-a- wah-to's.[1] Where was Green?

I ran along the ice-foot to meet the sledge. Yes, they were Pee-a-wah-to's dogs. As the question, "Where's Green?"

---

[1] In modern orthography the name is usually spelt Piugaattoq.

was about to burst from my lips, the driver, whose eyes were covered with large metal glasses, seemed to turn suddenly into a strange likeness of Green. He looked as if he had risen from the grave.

"This is all there is left of your southern division," he said.

Green had shot the hunter, in circumstances that were never properly explained. Green later claimed that the two had been caught in a blizzard and when it cleared Piugaattoq took the sled and said he was returning to Etah. Thinking he was being abandoned, Green grabbed a rifle and shot the man in the back. Desperate and without time to argue, MacMillan assumed that Green had misunderstood Piugaattoq and he took questions over the killing no further, though he did comment that Piugaattoq had been a reliable and uncomplaining guide on several Arctic expeditions, including Peary's.

Whether Green had committed manslaughter or murder, for Macmillan the killing of Piugaattoq was probably not the low point for the expedition. He would be trapped out in the Arctic for nearly four years. Team members would lose fingers and toes to frostbite, equipment would break down, two ships sent to rescue the expedition became themselves trapped in ice, and once they'd missed the brief window that the Arctic summer offered there'd be nine months of waiting for the waters to clear.

And yet, not long before the killing, MacMillan had witnessed a vision.

April 21st was a beautiful day; all mist was gone and the clear blue of the sky extended down to the very horizon. Green was no sooner out of the igloo than he came

22

running back, calling in through the door, "We have it!" Following Green, we ran to the top of the highest mound. There could be no doubt about it. Great heavens! What a land! Hills, valleys, snow- capped peaks extending through at least one hundred and twenty degrees of the horizon. I turned to Pee-a- wah-to anxiously and asked him toward which point we had better lay our course. After critically examining the supposed landfall for a few minutes, he astounded me by replying that he thought it was poo-jok (mist).

Piugaattoq's dismissal of the phenomenon explained, more importantly *confirmed* Peary's original sighting, though even today some writers charge Peary with inventing the land to extract more funding from the Arctic Club. But the poles have always been hallucinatory, where a quiet crack in the ice can echo for miles, sped along by a cold dryness unhampered by physical obstruction. And mirages are common. People see mysterious lakes and phantom islands so often they don't report them, but in the early nineteenth century Yakov Sannikov saw an island off Siberia and for decades Sannikov Land appeared on Russian maps. Peary didn't have to lie to get money from his backers. Men like George Crocker had enough to throw at him and were willing to do so.

Fitzhugh Green never had to lie either; inquiries into the death of Piugaattoq were willing to accept his version and its extenuating circumstances. In the 1920s he turned his hand to science fiction. In *ZR Wins*, a naval officer overhears some "Orientals" discussing a sinister plan and realizes what's at stake.

"London and Tokyo are on opposite sides of the Pole," he had explained. "They represent the gigantic markets of

Europe and Asia. Halfway between, in the unexplored area of the Polar Sea, may lie an unknown land."

An expedition is launched, not just to discover this unknown land but save Western Civilization in the process. The airship crashes, things look grim but rescue is at hand, by:

Blond Eskimos? But they couldn't be Eskimos, these tall, superbly-built and handsome men and women! Then flashed back the tale so often he had tried to make his friends believe. Tale of the Norsemen on the Greenland coast five centuries before. Happy, thriving, prosperous colonists. Abandoned without warning by the mother country…

An elderly man came forward. He was close to seven feet tall. His flowing hair and beard were white. His ruddy cheeks and piercing blue eyes, combined with the soft form-fitting shirt of brown wool that covered him to his knees, made him a striking figure. One could imagine him erect on the poop of a Viking ship, eyes shaded towards a new land that beckoned his kind ever on.

He spoke a few words in a strange tongue.

Then…there issued from the giant's lips a greeting in plain English, perfectly enunciated.

"Welcome, stranger. Do I now speak the language of your country?"

This from a man who'd been out there, who knew firsthand what real extremes the white emptiness and relentless cold pushed people to. You have to believe in karma to be influenced by it, and Green most likely didn't, but for a while his life looked immune to any payback for past actions. He rose in the ranks of the US Navy, becoming a Lieutenant Commander, wrote books of popular history on cinema and aviation, novels like *ZR Wins* and *The Mystery of the Erik*. And in 1933, he married Margery Durant, daughter of William Durant, founder of General Motors. Fitzhugh and Margery were a good match, both being adventurers (she had her pilot's licence in the 1930s), into photography and film and the social whirl of America's industrial cities. They were also into opiates, busted in 1947 and (very briefly) jailed. It sounds like cosmic revenge but to be fair, there were a lot of addicts after the war, though no one talked much about that. Drug addiction is a form of haunting, an incoherent obsession. And if *ZR Wins* has any sensible message it's that Green was also haunted by his time in the Arctic, in ways he preferred to keep hidden.

Explorers are supposed to find great things. That's the point to going out there; great things defined as those that change the way a culture thinks of itself. All the stories here are accounts of failure to comprehend that greatness, by the person who found it, by those that sent them out, or the society that demanded a retelling. That was never intentional. Only when it was complete was it possible to look at the thing as whole and see the glaringly obvious, the missing detail. How ever you look at the history of exploration, it is a history of human failure.

# CHAPTER 1

## Marguerite and the Isle of Demons

### The New World

The place to start this account of what happened on the Isle of Demons in the 1540s is not off the coast of Newfoundland, where everything happened, but in Rome some thirty years earlier. Imagine a monk's cell, with just enough space to stretch out the arms, a shelf stacked untidily with rolled up manuscripts and several bound volumes, a desk cluttered with compasses, squares and other drafting equipment, a crucifix above the desk, and a cat sleeping under it, there for company and to protect the manuscripts from mice. Here, Johannes Ruysch is constructing his map of the world.

The first stage of the project is a matter of gathering information from written reports, interviews, navigational charts and that public knowledge that circulates free of charge, and for that matter evidence or verification. During the second stage Ruysch applies all this to the construction of the outline of the known world: Europe, Asia, Africa and the recently discovered land mass known as the New World. Contemporaneously, in the Duchy of Lorraine, Martin Waldseemüller is creating his world map. He will label the land mass America, but for now Ruysch calls part of the northern half Terra Nova, the New World, and the larger, southern mass Terre Sancte Crucis, or Land of the Holy Cross. He does not depict them as connected, and Terra Nova is still an eastern coast of Asia.

Like all cartographers in this age of exploration, Ruysch loathes empty spaces; they represent ignorance and failure, so once he has completed the outline of a continent he fills the interior with mountains, forests and rivers. The North Pole is four islands: Aronphei (the furthest part north of the Earth), a desert island, Hyperborei Europa (most northern point of Europe, and land of the Hyperboreans) and another desert island, all of them ringed by a forbidding phalanx of mountain chains. According to his inscription, the North Pole is just that: a massive magnetic column surrounded by tempestuous seas that draws everything in and destroys it. His description can be doubted but not disproved; no one can get close enough to the pole to do that.

Elsewhere, he includes inscriptions describing places according to the latest information received. An archipelago off Newfoundland he calls Insula Baccalauras, from the Portuguese for islands of cod; in recent times the Portuguese have begun competing with the French and British for cod off these parts. His map is heavily reliant on Portuguese sources: the Portuguese are the most reliable according to some, his political masters according to others. But even the Portuguese can never be entirely trusted.

Of the Land of the Holy Cross he says:

The men and women go either entirely naked or wearing wood and brightly coloured feathers…they have no religion and no king and are constantly at war. They eat

27

the flesh of men they have captured in war: they live to be one hundred and fifty years old. When they are sick they take roots or herbs as cures. Lions are here, and serpents and other foul beasts. There are forests, mountains and rivers, and an abundance of pearls and gold.

And so on; barely fifteen years after Columbus's first voyage, nothing here so incredible to beggar belief, but as with all breaking news it awaits confirmation.

Off the coast between Greenland and Newfoundland is a tiny island, which on his map is really two separated by a narrow stream. It is insignificant; just like the inland mountains and forests on the continents it appears to be there to fill in space, but Ruysch writes:

Others have claimed that those who came before in ships to these islands for fish and other food were attacked by the demons so that they could not land without danger.

It is an oddly ambiguous statement from a cartographer otherwise willing to vouch for any myth if it sounds extravagant enough. Firstly, it deflects responsibility to unknown others, then he suggests that if there were encounters with demons they happened in the past, though on that point it's a matter of translation; he could also be saying that people who have been to the island in the past have reported such things. And then he fails to mention that he may have been one of those people, on John Cabot's 1497 voyage.

Cabot was attempting a reconsideration of Columbus's expedition, to find a route to Asia but across the top, through what would later become known as the North West Passage. He was also searching for the magical island of Hy-Brasil off the

Irish coast, said to emerge from the mist once every seven years. And there were rumours from fishermen to look into, that out past the fishing grounds lay lands dense with forests. This determination to regard fact and belief as equally plausible, or the inability to distinguish between the two, lay at the core of the era of exploration. Perhaps that is the explanation for Ruysch's equivocation: he has seen enough to understand the difference. Having been out there, he knows that if the mysterious Hy-Brasil does exist it will most likely be like the other islands out there that he passed: sunless, dreary and barren, about as magical a place as a village jail.

## The Island of Demons

The ship sits with drooping sails, a discarded carcass in the still, grey water. One after the other, the two women and the man climb unsteadily down the rope ladder and into the rowboat, where six oarsmen wait ready to cast off. Their few possessions, wrapped in bundles, are lowered down and as each parcel reaches the boat one of the sailors hands them to the older woman and the man. The three passengers sit wrapped in blankets, heads bowed. Leaning over the bulwark, the ship's captain gives a nod and the sailors dip their oars. The boat pulls away from the ship, towards a shadowy landform wreathed in cold, damp fog.

It is 1542. The figure on the deck watching the rowboat disappear into the mist is Jean-François de Roberval, captain of an expedition of two hundred French colonists, most of them convicts, intending to support the new settlement of Charlesbourg-Royal on the Saint Lawrence River. Portraits tend to depict de Roberval with a troubled expression, though whether that's from the immediate task at hand or something more profound it is difficult to say. This voyage has already given him enough reason to feel pessimistic. The plan had been to join Jacques Cartier at Charlesbourg-Royal, but a few days earlier the ships had met off Newfoundland. Cartier was now on his way back to France to show the King the chests of glittering iron pyrites he'd found scattered on the ground, and which he believed were proof that the new colony was rich in precious metals.

The encounter with Cartier and his fool's gold foreshadowed the expedition's entrance into the Gulf of Saint Lawrence. Occasional glimpses of the shore suggested a drab, grey world. Even in late May, when French gardens were coming into bloom, the clouded sky and drizzle was as bleak as a Breton December.

Fog has a way of amplifying sound and de Roberval can hear the slap of the oars on the water long after the boat has vanished from view. He remains on deck and won't move until the six oarsmen return. Of their three passengers, the older woman will be known only as Damienne, and the man simply as the Lover. The younger woman, she is in her early twenties, will be known to historians by a couple of names. Sometimes she will be called Marguerite de la Rocque, sometimes Marguerite de Roberval. She is the Captain's niece. A couple of days ago he discovered (inevitable on a ship this size) she was having an affair with one of the sailors. Showing impressive rectitude for a man who'd spent the last five years raiding Spanish ships, de Roberval felt he had no choice but to cast the two malefactors and her nursemaid on to the island to fend for themselves. To show he wasn't completely heartless, he gave them an arquebus for a weapon, some tools and enough food for them to get started with their new lives.

Before long, the only sound from the direction the rowboat had headed into was the spectral cry of gannets circling above the grey landform marked on maps as the Isle of Demons.

Despite the paucity of hard evidence – at best a couple of official documents that may include her name – Marguerite's existence is accepted. This is because she survived her ordeal on the Isle of Demons to be interviewed by two people of somewhat impeccable credentials: one a fabulist, the other an ideologue. Both treated her story as a tabula rasa on which they could inscribe their own ideas of history, mores and gender, but they were not to be challenged on their subject's credibility: the fabulist was one of France's most respected geographers and the ideologue was the Queen of Navarre.

There can doubt about everything else though, even the location of the Isle of Demons. Sixteenth century cartographers were uncertain, or more likely not especially fussed about where they located it. According to some interpretations it is present day Belle Island, halfway between Labrador and the island of Newfoundland, but Quirpon and other smaller islands nearby have been proposed. What matters here is, like Marguerite's story, not so much the facts but their possibility. The Isle of Demons sounds like the fading echo of a medieval legend, a rocky outcrop where sailors were cast up on to do battle with

Satan's henchmen. It is nothing of the sort. By sixteenth century ideas it was a very modern place.

Those devil haunted islands of the past were always located further south, near the Azores or the Canary Islands. In their time they represented the edge of European knowledge, beyond which all remained vague and unsettling. This Isle of Demons, where Marguerite and her companions were dumped, made its first official appearance on Ruysch's 1508 world map. Like all world maps of the period, his was less a visual representation of the Earth than a survey of current knowledge, which, only sixteen years after Columbus's first voyage, was still admittedly meagre. On Ruysch's map, Newfoundland extended westwards to join up with Asia, so Tibet was just a short cruise south around the coast (roughly where New York now stands). Ruysch could hardly be blamed for these errors. A priest, it had been years since he had sailed past the Isle of Demons; in the interim he'd been stricken with tuberculosis and could not return, so he stayed in Rome with his adventurous past and a receding memory, creating maps that relied on information others passed to him.

Contemporary Protestant thought allowed for a place that could be inhabited by demons, but the scholars preferred to think in metaphoric terms: evil may happen there but ideally at the hands of men, not horned homunculi. The proposition that Breton fishermen heard the unearthly chatter of roosting gannets and imagined that the fog hid an island of supernatural creatures, was itself based on experience rather than speculation. Sailors, who still feared nature and God on even terms, entered this part of the world with trepidation, and hearing the racket from thousands of seabirds roosting on the cliffs assumed the source to be demons furiously swirling about. To the scholars, the sailors had the facts but not the ability to interpret them properly.

But wherever exactly the Isle of Demons was, it lay in a dead zone, on the same latitude as Bristol, where in the years before Columbus, most of the English fishing boats set out for the Newfoundland fishing grounds from. There was nothing between Bristol and Newfoundland as the crow flies except the open sea. Climatically speaking, however, they were poles apart.

Though Greenland and the Arctic hung ominously above both, Bristol had Ireland to protect it from the high winds and low temperatures coursing south. Belle and Quirpon Island on the other hand faced the Labrador Sea and the Davis Strait, a channel funneling the very worst of the polar weather towards it. To add further misery to that, the North Atlantic Deep Water Mass lay just off shore. This enormous bowl of very cold water sits close to the warm Gulf Stream, directing the weather so that in the summer, damp cool air skating across the water's surface creates a form of advection fog, while in the winter the cold air meeting the water creates an evaporation fog.

Which is to say that fog is the natural condition of the region. Inhabitants describe standing at the edge of the land on clear days and watching a bank of white clouds barreling across the water towards them like a tsunami, which can, as though by divine intervention, dissipate just before colliding with the land. Fog has other tricks. It can distort sounds so the listener can't tell which direction they are coming from, and it can amplify them, so a gentle noise like the creak of a distant windmill's arms can sound as though it is right by the listener's ear.

Fog smothers sunlight, weakening its power to give life. It has ruined the topography of these islands. There are no real trees, just stunted and withered facsimiles clinging to lichen encrusted rock. Grasses and sedges survive best, doggedly unruffled by the damp fog and cold wind. Barren and desolate are the wrong words for this gloomy environment; nihilistic captures its soulless, unfeeling atmosphere better.

Within a few weeks of being stranded Marguerite knew she was pregnant. It isn't recorded whether the Lover survived long enough to witness the birth, or to help bury the baby. Damienne also died quickly, leaving Marguerite alone on the island. Soon after she had dug the grave of the last of her companions, the demons who inhabited the island began persecuting her, circling her little camp during the night and screaming at her, refusing to let her sleep. She never encountered one physically, but sometimes at dusk in the corner of her eye she'd catch sight of them flitting about the branches of the trees. When she moved into a cave to find shelter from the brutal winter cold, they hovered about outside, wailing and cackling, waiting for her to re-emerge.

She wasn't safe once the sun came up either. The demons became excited at first light, just before the wild animals emerged. Grim, hungry lions and wolves with blood slathered jaws prowled the landscape. Peering through the fog, she'd glimpse their bulky, formless shadows and hear their low throated growls on the wind.

Because her audience knew next to nothing about the New World, it was easy to imagine it inhabited by the most terrifying creatures, but even the most gullible might have asked themselves how much of what she saw was real and how much the creation of frayed nerves. The toughest nuts will crack under sufficient strain, and what she had to endure would have broken most people.

One morning Marguerite left the safety of the cave in her daily forage for food and ran into a massive, snarling bear.

That part of her story was probably true.

## The Queen and the Geographer

Marguerite, Queen of Navarre was dying; cancer, probably, but whatever the diagnosis, her slow demise came as no surprise to her. She'd had intimations in dreams and visions for some time now. Throughout her life she'd encountered people who had passed to the other side: husbands, her children, brothers, friends, and she was not afraid of death, only that it would take her before her great project was complete.

This was a work something between a history, an encyclopaedia and a courtesy book, on the matter of women, on how they should love, and who, and why. Like the most famous example of that type, Christina de Pizan's *The Book of the City of Ladies*, Marguerite de Navarre's *Heptaméron* was constructed as a complex series of self-contained allegories drawn from history and her own inquiries, which is to say that she cared little for facts but everything for the truth.

Borrowing from another Renaissance classic, Boccaccio's *Decameron*, Queen Marguerite arranged her work to be sequences of ten stories told over ten days, by travellers lodging in an abbey while a bridge is being built. Boccaccio saw his book as a reflection of the tapestry of humanity: its venality and corruption, dignity and courage, sometimes in the same person. Christine de Pizan imagined a world where women assumed authority because they accepted responsibility: history as analogy. In Queen Marguerite's, women were permitted to be submissive, even servile if the outcome was a moral triumph. She viewed the world as broken, and only the most authentic love could put it right.

*The Spanish story of Florida, who, after withstanding the love of a gentleman named Amadour for many years, eventually becomes a nun,* or, *Praiseworthy artifice of a lady to whom a sea captain sent a letter and diamond ring, and who, by forwarding them to the captain's wife as though they had been intended for her, united husband and wife once more in all affection,* or *How the Lady of Loué regained her husband's affection* sat among tales of commonplace heartbreak and revenge, each a revelation concerned with life's choices and how they play out. One day, about 1545 or 1546, at a time when the unsettled dreams and shortness of breath were already reminding her she had no time to waste, another Marguerite was presented to her.

This Marguerite had achieved a kind of fame, on account of being rescued from the sinister Isle of Demons by a passing fishing boat a couple of years earlier. The bones of her story, inchoate and barely credible, were nevertheless riven with a fascinating horror. Night after night for almost a year she had wedged herself into her small cave and fought off hordes of swooping demons. By day she had ventured out into the mist strewn landscape to forage for food, aware of the ghostly shadows of loping predators. All this while grieving for the loss of her infant, and perhaps her lover.

In the cold reason of Queen Marguerite's passion, this other Marguerite represented a vague but profound space between victimization and self-sacrifice. She had defied her uncle no less and followed her paramour on to the island, and when he had died she had struggled on alone, transcending the mere nobility of altruism to discover wellsprings within of courage and resistance.

Queen Marguerite had her own losses, her own struggles, but they shriveled in comparison to this Marguerite, who had faced hers alone, with what appeared to be little more than faith in the Lord, and in her own will.

Novel LXVII of the *Heptaméron*; *Love and extreme hardships of a woman in a foreign land*, opened with the voyage to the Island of Canada, where on the crossing de Roberval discovered "among whom there was one who was base enough to betray his master, so that he was near falling into the hands of the natives".

With swift recourse, de Roberval had a noose thrown over a yard arm, and prepared to have the traitor hanged, and:

He would have done so but for the wife of this wretch, who, after sharing the perils of the sea with her husband, was willing to follow his bad fortune to the end. She prevailed so far by her tears and supplications, that Robertval (sic), both for the services she had rendered him, and from compassion for her, granted what she asked. This was, that her husband and herself should be left on a little island in the sea, inhabited only by wild beasts, with permission to take with them what was necessary for their subsistence.

With arquebus in one hand and Bible in the other, Marguerite learned to hunt wild animals for food but, with her companions dying in quick order and left alone, her only comfort lay in prayers and songs of praise. The sailors who found her a year later could not believe she had survived so long on such piddling sustenance, but she pointed to her Bible with its now broken spine and loose pages.

No mention in any of this that the (unnamed) wife in the story was de Roberval's niece; that might have spoiled the effect. After all, what kind of man would cast his own blood on a deserted island without just cause? But then, there was no mention of demons either. Queen Marguerite was interested in the human power of love, which could be influenced by fortune or will but never divine intervention. In her world, a woman could sacrifice everything for a man and lose it all yet emerge somehow triumphant in the end. So, her story gave only a fleeting nod to what evidence Marguerite de Roberval had presented, so much of that clearly contrary to the Queen's determined plan. She set out to depict the castaway in the role of the vulnerable wife of a man too willing to trade the lives of his crewmates for a paltry sum. The real story, the Queen was arguing, was the castaway's transformation from clinging dependent to self-reliant heroine, a woman full of weeping anxieties developing into someone fierce and resolute. Mortal love lay at the beginning and the end of that, so out went the demons and any other distractions.

"Now, ladies," Queen Marguerite closed her moral fable with sound advice for an age stricken with spiritual doubt and fear. "You cannot say but that I laud the virtues which God has implanted in you – virtues which appear the greater, the weaker the being that displays them."

Here her lesson ended.

Such subtle uncertainties did not concern Andre Thevét. He knew that if anybody ever questioned his claims about the New World, he only had to look them in the eye and ask, "have you been there?"

Hardly anyone in Europe had, even by the time he was compiling his encyclopaedic description during the 1570s. Among those few, the ones who'd survived and returned with a story to tell, most weren't fit to be believed in the first place, being common soldiers or seamen, or criminals who'd been sent to colonies like New France because their death would be no great loss, economically or socially.

Thevét was a Franciscan friar, which marked him by custom as a mendicant and man of humility, but also open to visions of God's wonder. If the Jesuits were God's soldiers, the Franciscans were the mystic fundamentalists, embracing an ascetic position terrifying to all but the mad and the powerful. More importantly, Thevét was a cosmographer. He did not simply consider the Earth and its physical shape but its place in the universe, divine or otherwise. A cartographer, like Ruysch, depended upon mundane testimony from others. A cosmographer could dispense with that if his power of reason was superior. He could imagine spheres within spheres, extending to the edges of the universe (which were not that far away), itself ringed with fire, or even something more solid, a crust of ice or brown soil; so long as the description sounded convincing, and theology permitted it. What all this meant: the mysticism, the visions, the fundamentalism, is that facts were not sacred.

In 1555 Thevét joined an expedition to Brazil as its chaplain. Within days of arrival, he was laid low with fever and after a couple of months was shipped back to France. He'd viewed the New World through a window adjacent to his hospital bed.

Readers of his account of his travels, *Les Singularitez de la France antarctique* would have been none the wiser. His descriptions of Brazil and of North America as far up as Newfoundland had the ring of veracity. This was not because Thevét had an especially persuasive style, or that the majority of his readers had never left Europe so could not contradict him. His success lay in understanding what they wanted to hear.

Brazil may have been a rancid jungle, and its inhabitants unwelcoming, but it had prospects; stories of hidden wealth were enough to lure in adventurers. Brazil, in the scheme of things, was considered a Portuguese possession. New France, up where Marguerite de Navarre had called the Island of Canada, was, of course, French. The closest Thevét came to New France may have been Bermuda, but even that was unlikely. Nevertheless, in sharp contrast to the jungle dwelling Brazilians, up that way the inhabitants were gentle, kind and quite sophisticated. He thought the deerskin outfits the women wore were better than those available in France, and the men marched into battle in a structured formation to the sounds of drums and flutes.

Scholars of early European contact with North America have dedicated careers to reading Thevét closely, wondering how to interpret someone who mixed obscure fact (how could he know the people of New France wore snowshoes unless he had been there?) with preposterous fabrications (after only a couple of weeks communicating with the inhabitants, he had enough vocabulary to produce a lexicon). Let philosophers wear themselves out worrying about the boundaries between truth and fable. Evidently, like Marguerite de Navarre, Thevét regarded himself as a novelist, someone who spun scraps of information, common knowledge or life experience into a grand narrative. His grandest was the *Cosmographie Universelle*, a massive digest of everything that was known about the world in the 1570s, according to Andre Thevét that is. Here he talked about the Isle of Demons for the first time:

> ...the one they call [Isle] of the Demons, which is the largest and most beautiful. [is] at present uninhabited because of the great illusions and phantoms which are seen there, through the trickery and deceit of the devils. This has also been experienced even by Christians and that is why they gave it this name of Isle of Demons, or devils, as is said – and it is a great pity considering the beauty of the place and that it is closer to us than any of the others. People go there fairly often in the daytime for fishing and hunting: but if you get too far inland you will not fail to meet up with these accursed spirits, which make a thousand assaults on you in the woods and lonely spots in broad daylight.

Thevét had studied Ruysch's map closely, and all the others that followed where the Isle of Demons appeared. Some of these had repeated Ruysch's idea of the divided island, which allowed for one half to be dominated by devils and the other by angels, but generally the argument was over precise location. Sometimes it was north of the entrance to the Saint Lawrence River, sometimes well to the east. In his 1570 map Abraham Ortelius, Gerhard Mercator's rival for the claim as Europe's greatest cartographer, placed it close to Iceland, not far from Frisland and Saint Brendan's Isle, and just south of Estotiland on the Canadian coast, a land ruled by a king who owned a library of books in Latin. The doubtful creator of the late 1550s Pseudo-Agnese map placed the Isle of Demons up in the far north. In its contours it bore a strong resemblance to the outline of Britain, and only slightly smaller, though this was probably a failure of imagination of the cartographer's part rather than a deliberate political statement.

If only the number of claims as to the existence of something amount to a proof, then the maps were all Thevét needed, but because he considered himself a scholar, and a pragmatist, he was drawn to those places on maps marked as ruled by mythical kings, rumoured to have mountains sparkling with gems, or islands inhabited by demons. In the 1570s it was possible to study a map of the world with its approximate outlines and empty interiors and believe there was still space for such things, just as it was possible to persuade princes and government officials they were worth searching for.

The people best able to vouch for those stories were the same who could never be trusted: ordinary sailors and fishermen. Thevét sought them out and gave their accounts the same weight of respectability as those of priestly mapmakers. Elsewhere, he said that he'd interviewed Marguerite de Roberval at her family home in the Perigord.

He should have; it was after all his professional duty. By the 1560s he was cosmographer at the court of Charles IX, which not only gave him access to travellers but obliged them to present themselves for interrogation. Anyone who had taken the now well-worn road to China, or sailed down the African coast, or claimed for whatever dubious motive that they had returned from the court of Prester John, was obliged to come in for an interview. A woman who had lived alone at the very edge of the known world, in parts so hostile that small armies of men were afraid to enter them, would not have escaped his attention.

The questions he asked were not recorded but he knew Jean-François de Roberval and must have been aware that Queen Marguerite had met Marguerite de Roberval. *The Heptaméron* had been published in 1558 (almost ten years after Queen Marguerite's death) and even if Thevét found the rest of the book too pious in its advocacy of women, the single detail that this woman of minor nobility had been in Canada, on the Isle of Demons no less, was enough for him to demand her presence.

There is no record either of how Marguerite de Roberval felt when the interview finally ended. Perhaps it was as many have ever since, when a subject has been seduced by a reporter hiding self-interest behind wide-eyed fascination. If she ever read Thevét's account, she must have wondered how her story became so grotesquely twisted.

The only innocent person in it was Jean-François de Roberval. No surprises there as the two men knew each other. But more importantly for Thevét's reputation, the expedition to colonise Canada was undertaken on the orders of the King. To impugn de Roberval was to imply the King's judgement was poor.

> Roberval...having equipped himself as required for entry into this country through the liberality of his prince, and also employing a good part of his own wealth, took with him a good company of gentlemen and artisans of all kinds and several women: among others a Damoiselle who was a rather close relative of his, named Marguerite, whom he greatly respected and to whom he confided all his affairs since she was of his blood.

The betrayal was already etched in those last words. No reason to mention that he'd taken her into his confidences unless she was about to betray them. Mutiny was one thing but to be turned on by your own family was another. Soon enough, under circumstances lightly skipped over, de Roberval discovers his beloved niece is carrying on with one of the crewmen. The precise cause of the offence is not mentioned either. Was she entrusted to his care, or was there an unmentioned familial animus, a transgression of class boundaries between Marguerite and the Lover, something else inexplicable or unutterable? Thevét was not interested. In any case, a bitter but justified de Roberval packed the two lovers off to the island. He:

> disguised his wrath, which he conceived more against his relative than against the gentleman...There Roberval left them, angry at the wrong his relative had done them and joyous at having punished them without soiling his hands with their blood.

Having protected France's honour, so far as Thevét is concerned, Roberval sails off to continue his mission, leaving Marguerite, the Lover and Damienne on the island, where:

> They killed a lot of animals, whose meat they ate, and lived off fruits, for of bread they had no way to have any. But it was a pity to hear the ravages which those evil spirits made around them and how they tried to destroy their little dwelling, appearing as divers kinds and shapes of frightful animals. But [they were] finally vanquished by the constancy and perseverance of these Christians, contrite over their sins, and did not afflict or trouble them any more except that at night they often heard such loud cries that it seemed as if there were more than 100,000 men together.

Queen Marguerite claimed only to be interested in simple moral questions. Thevét insisted that no matter how incredible the stories he recounted, they were only there to further scientific knowledge. Queen Marguerite's castaway began life on the island as a weak and fragile young lady, while Thevét's was a scheming Jezebel, yet both authors were basically telling the same story, of how a young woman alone and facing apparently insurmountable challenges overcame them through strength of character. For Queen Marguerite the secret lay in unswerving faith, for Thevét it was her resourcefulness: a bible in one hand, a gun in the other.

# A Bear as White as an Egg

As the sun rose over the island and its rays trickled insipidly through the fog, the demons shrank away and the beasts emerged.

These fascinated Thevét. Fantastic beasts defined the world beyond the known, and even if the creatures he was likely to have encountered in Brazil were vaguely familiar to someone who had travelled to North Africa, he illustrated his *Cosmographie* with unicorns, sea monsters and undefined mammals with distinctly human faces. They represented a fervent hope that those parts of the globe awaiting discovery would turn out to be more fabulous that ordinary imagination allowed.

The bear that attacked Marguerite, that she fought off with bullets or fists or even screams, was "as white as an egg".

"And of the bear that attacked you?" Thevét would have wanted to know that, but the way he framed it and the question that followed would have defined the entire interview. Would he have asked, "what colour was it?", and let her speak, or would he have already decided: "was it white?"

That description, "white as an egg", has the ring of experience rather than learning. Thevét may never have been further north than the Netherlands but in all his reading, and close examination of maps – Martin Behaim's 1492 globe, the Erdapfel, or Olaus Magnus's 1539 *Carta marina*, or Pierre Desceliers' 1550 map – he would have seen polar bears. (The Desceliers map had bears on islands off Labrador, close by other islands inhabited by elephants.) He had never needed to see one to know they existed, but also, if a bear turned up on the Isle of

Demons, he knew it was north enough to be white. Marguerite de Roberval on the other hand may have seen women at the French court wearing coats imported from Russia and Scandinavia that were trimmed with polar bear fur, but she was unlikely to be as familiar with the zoology of the Arctic as Thevét.

What neither of them would have known (microscopes were not yet invented) was that the polar bear's fur is not white but translucent, the whiteness enhanced by the effect of resting against black hide and reflections from the snow. And it is never pure but a dirty white, closer sometimes to yellow, or, for someone reaching for a comparison, especially someone whose world till now was centred on the domestic, the colour of a hen's egg. If it were Marguerite de Roberval who offered the description in other words, she was speaking from personal experience.

Wherever precisely it was, the Isle of Demons was within the range of the sixteenth century polar bear's habitat. Helped by the brief cooling known as the mini ice-age that began around 1500, the polar bear would have found the coasts down to Nova Scotia a lavish source of fish and seal meat, and if it were late spring and the seasonal thaw had set in, a curious, or even a slow-witted bear could have jumped on a passing ice-floe and found itself beached on the Isle of Demons. Not just one bear: Queen Marguerite talked of wild beasts as though the island teemed with them, and Thevét was more specific, Marguerite the castaway fought off at least three bears, though only one described as white.

What then of the demons? In his abstruse way, Thevét let it be known that he never really believed in them. He liked the idea of their existence and would have preferred an island inhabited by actual agents of Satan to something more rational (such as gannets), but the way he avoided any physical description, or commitment to their existence, made his scepticism apparent. Being a scholar monk, he also employed that contradictory sophistry the Church encouraged, to insist its followers maintained belief in the supernatural while treating any personal encounters they had as highly dubious.

Queen Marguerite had not mentioned demons, unless she equated them with wild beasts. Not that she was more practical or less imaginative than Thevét, her island after all was inhabited by lions, but the persecution Marguerite the castaway suffered always welled from within. This was something a woman subject to conversations with dead relatives and friends would understand, not as a form of madness but a curse nevertheless. Think of an island, even one that is nothing more than a strip of sand with a single palm tree on it, occupy it alone, and before long the demons will arrive. Marguerite de Roberval's hymns and prayers weren't just attempts to converse with the Lord, she was trying to drown out the chatter constantly attacking her sanity.

One day, sighting a ship passing by, Marguerite de Roberval crawled down to the beach and attempted to signal it. Keen-eyed sailors suddenly remembered the three castaways left on the island back when the expedition was about to enter the Saint Lawrence River. A boat was lowered and she was rescued. She answered the question of how she had survived, as we saw earlier, by showing the sailors her little cave, the scraps of food littering the floor and her deteriorated bible.

Of the woman who sat down with Queen Marguerite and later Andre Thevét, a desire to see loose ends made neat requires that she was restored to full health, that by the time of the interviews the last of the demons had been silenced and she faced her questioners with the serene elegance instilled in a woman raised in the French court. Logic warns against that. Neither the Queen nor the geographer could care less about the real Marguerite sitting before them: more to the point it was in their interests to ignore her. Who, after all, would want to tell the tale of a woman finding strength in faith, only to discover she was a burnt-out shell? Likewise, to hear her tales of encounters with demons only to realise she had been driven irrevocably mad from her stay on the island would have established beyond doubt how ludicrous the legends were. Better for both to overlook any contrary evidence and stick to the story they were determined to tell.

So Marguerite de Roberval told her story, twice, then vanished, leaving even less of a record than before.

## Myths and Monsters

In early portraits, Marguerite of Navarre wears velvet gowns and heavy pendants and holds a parrot, a symbol of the Virgin Mary. The later portraits show a woman in simpler dress, with keen but tired eyes, much as we'd assume in a writer aware of her mortality. Sometimes she holds a spaniel pup, an acknowledgement that though she was a princess of France, Navarre had been conquered by the Spanish. Throughout her life she was depicted as learned, politically engaged and pious. But court artists were not employed to tell the truth, far from it. Every portrait was an assertion about power and physical likenesses were subsumed under the political statement. Because of that, whatever her age, Marguerite of Navarre looks like all royal women in sixteenth century portraits: she could also be Anne Boleyn or Catherine de Medici, a Prussian duchess or a Spanish infanta. So often, what we are being asked to read into the portraits is based on our assumptions.

The same could be said of Andre Thevét, whose face in several woodcuts is so different that it is difficult to believe they are the same man. As with Marguerite de Navarre, the identification of the sitter rests in the supporting apparatus, in his case usually a globe, or a pair of dividers, or a palm tree.

Of Marguerite the castaway there are no surviving portraits, which is how it should be. She is a cypher for anyone who wants to impose their story on to hers.

In what is probably the earliest depiction of her, a picture of the island that appeared in Thevét's *Cosmographie Universelle*, two bears menace her from behind a palm tree. Unfazed, she is pointing her gun at them. Behind her, a baby sleeps beside a neatly made grass hut. Various small figures, demons presumably, flitter about. Elsewhere on the island there are plenty of trees, and deer, and a scorpion, to remind the viewer that this little tropical paradise in the Arctic north still held dangers.

Thevét probably drew the map himself, so it was in keeping with his opinion of himself that he belonged to a tradition that began as far back as Herodotus and Pliny and included Marco

Polo and John Mandeville. He had a responsibility to report wonders and marvels, whether or not he believed in them. Hence, the island included images of things he had been told about, which was not the same as saying he held them to be true.

That scene of Marguerite fighting off the polar bear would become the most vivid image of her account. During the 1870s, Godefroy Durand (probably) illustrated an article about her with a wonderfully Victorian idea of the New Woman. The plucky and (more importantly) elegantly dressed Marguerite blasts away at point blank range at one bear while another lies dead at its feet. Behind her stands a thick, mountainous pine forest. Adventurer and explorer, she has become a cross between the outlaw Belle Starr and the traveller Isabella Bird.

Nothing could be so further from that than the illustration accompanying the 1894 English edition of the *Heptaméron*. Here Marguerite sits under a palm tree, beside another well-constructed grass hut, reading her bible to the Lover. He is dying; we know this because although he wears his uniform, he is slumped and holding a crucifix. Though the records state the castaways were given at least one arquebus, as mentioned previously, it was a particularly ungainly weapon, more cannon than gun. In this image, they have a long-barreled flintlock. Significantly, it rests against the hut beside the Lover's sword, indicating that he is the hunter, the hero. Evidently, Marguerite will fulfill her proper duty and continue to care for him until his last breath.

This is why no one has ever seriously disputed the story of Marguerite. Her elusiveness allowed her to become a heroine for all types in all ages: martyr, explorer, adventurer, caregiver. In the early days, before the railway and the telegraph, she was an ideal Canadian pioneer woman, spirited and self-reliant, able to fend off attacks by polar bears single-handed. Simultaneously she was also a French heroine; putting up ferocious resistance yet never losing her grace or poise. But then, her story, which without embellishment was still remarkable in an age when women of minor ranking were expected to be submissive, was exploited from the start.

Though neither Queen Marguerite nor Thevét gave a moment's care for what she told them, their stories already decided, the accounts were so different that it begs a question who was closer to the truth.

For Thevét, the problem lay with Jean-François; how to depict him as a leader worthy of an expedition into the unknown yet capable of abandoning his niece in the wilderness? The best way that could work was for Marguerite to betray him so her exile would be cruel but deserved. So, furious at discovering his niece carrying on an affair, Jean-François casts her off the ship. There were still problems with this basic plot. The most fundamental was that the entire purpose of the voyage was to colonise a part of the New World for France. All such ventures were fraught, and the record shows numerous efforts that failed. Only a few years later, the English colony at Roanoke in North Carolina would disappear without trace, or any answer ever since of what happened. Other colonies were abandoned as the settlers became ill, or failed to adapt to new conditions. In those circumstances, farmers, carpenters and other tradesmen were necessary, but to become established and grow, colonies depended upon women. In cold-blooded economic terms, being of child-bearing age, Marguerite was much too valuable to leave on an island to die.

The Lover could go. Like all the men on this voyage, he was expendable. Queen Marguerite was closer to the truth when she had de Roberval confront the Lover and banish him from the ship. There could be all kinds of reasons though an obvious one would be that Jean-François believed the man wasn't up to standards expected for his niece. Having decided to cast the Lover off, a common punishment, de Roberval had to deal with Marguerite suddenly insisting that she intended to join him.

For love to be pure it must also be reckless. The technical problem for Marguerite de Navarre was that she required passionate loyalty on the part of the woman but also a chasteness only a wife ought to have. The Queen could not allow Marguerite de Roberval to be some bored passenger. Nor could she permit the pair to be illicit lovers either; that would have placed Marguerite in the role of temptress, or at the least, accomplice. One way out of that trap was to make the man a traitor. Now the woman was so dutiful she was even prepared to follow a craven lowlife into exile. As a plot device, that solved all the important stumbling blocks. Young Marguerite's impetuous desire carried a terrible price, but through courage and devotion she would find redemption.

As the boat carrying the castaways draws nearer, the island begins to resolve itself into grey cliff faces speckled with shrivelled yellow scrub. The wind, even on this day in early summer, has a damp chill in it. Then there is that unearthly chatter that floats around them, never revealing its source. The gannet is the same dirty white colour as the polar bear, though with a black bandit's mask around its turquoise eyes, which suits it, being a bird that delights in its capacity for obnoxious behaviour. It likes to set off in the morning in gangs, prowling the seas and dive-bombing on to schools of fish like delinquent teenagers out to upset as much as survive. But its most offensive trait is that raucous, arrhythmic squawk. Coming from the gullet of one bird it sounds harsh enough, like listening to a rusted gate in the wind, but when thousands have gathered to roost, to mate, brood or wait for the seasonal shoals of fish, the effect is uncanny, and chilling in that way that only a racket with a perfectly mundane explanation can be. If logic says it cannot come from demons, for the human intruders the only other possibilities are every bit as terrifying.

The birds of course care nothing for what people think. They have been arriving on this island every spring for so long that instinct is now their only driving force. They are here to screech and flap their wings, chase off rivals, regurgitate sardines into their chicks' mouths, scream at their neighbours and defecate on their roosts and otherwise carry on in ways that only unbridled freedom allows. The sudden presence of three people on the island would be one of those events that become so rapidly absorbed into their frantically histrionic routines it will be acknowledged if at all by a mere handful nearby, who will make a momentary alteration in the tone of their squawks.

With a drop in the temperature towards the end of September, the gannets will become restless, gathering the strength for the long flight south to Mexico. Until then they head out each morning in search of the tell-tale glint of sardines and anchovies upon the water. Once the fish are spotted, they soar up to gain momentum then hurl themselves downward like a hellion army, craning their necks and drawing their bodies in to slice through the surface tension of the water with torpedo accuracy. They can do this for hours if necessary, returning to land with the sun's descent to disgorge part of their day's hunting into their chicks' mouths. Family responsibilities done with, they join the rest of the colony in their relentlessly strident, exuberantly abandoned chorus. Nature is crass, boorish and joyous.

# CHAPTER 2

## The Long-Forgotten Journey of David Ingram

*There is not any history in the world (the most holy writ accepted)*
*whereof we are precisely bound to believe each word and syllable.*
– Richard Hakluyt, *Voyages and Discoveries*, 1589.

## Mortlake I

The one thing people never forget about John Dee is that in the 1580s, while he was trying to communicate with angels, he met a forger named Edward Kelley who convinced him the two should share everything, especially their wives. It was exactly the evidence Dee's enemies at Queen Elizabeth's court were looking for, not because of any prurience on their part but because it proved he was a fool. Even today, people see their point. Everything else about Dee, his reputation as an antiquarian, his brief, brilliant career in the theatre building giant flying beetles, his role as court astrologer, essentially the spiritual advisor to Queen Elizabeth, his research into alchemy, and especially his original vision for an English empire spreading across the seas, that all gets brushed aside for the cuckold.

Often pinned as Shakespeare's model for the ageing and exiled Prospero in *The Tempest*, the two shared similar torments, though Prospero's banishment was physical while Dee was allowed to live in England and endure the contempt of men with lesser minds. Back in the Autumn of 1582 however, things were still going well at his house in Mortlake, a village on the Thames outside of London. Surrounded by his books and manuscripts, his inquiries into the language of the angels were making progress while his reputation as an astrologer and alchemist placed him among the leading thinkers of the age. His recent manuscript, *General and rare memorials pertayning to the Perfect art of Navigation*, an argument for establishing British colonies on the American coast as a step towards building a global English dominion, a *British empire* as he called it, had caught the attention of Queen Elizabeth's spymaster, Francis Walsingham, and merchants like George Peckham. Even Elizabeth travelled out to his house to consult with him personally. His library held the most extensive collection of works on cosmography, alchemy and the occult in the land.

Around three in the afternoon on July 6, 1582, George Peckham visited, wondering whether there could be any English claim to Norumbega. That was the land on the North American coast, southwest of the Isle of Demons and below the River of Torments. It had first appeared on maps about a century earlier, and though no one had found it yet, that was only a matter of time, so it still turned up, sometimes with features like rivers and bays already named. If John Dee found the English had a legitimate claim, he could be in for a handsome reward, five thousand acres in the New World, and just to show his goodwill, Peckham would send him a copy of Mercator's new map.

Five months later, on November 1, 1582, Dee had four visitors, which he entered the record in his diary as just another day of meetings and consultations.

> Nov.1st, Mr. Plat, my brother Yonghis sonne-in-law, cam to me with a stranger of Trushen, born at Regius Mons: his name is Martinus Faber. The same day cam Mr. Clement the seamaster and Mr. Ingram from Sir George Peckham.

Regius Mons was the Latin translation of Konigsberg, a Prussian port on the Baltic. Today it is Kaliningrad in Russia. Whoever preferred the Latin, Dee or Faber, the choice indicated the visitor was a scholar and that the discussion was about serious, somewhat cerebral issues. The second meeting was given such a cursory acknowledgement that the reader might think two neighbours dropped in for tea, but if George Peckham was right, David Ingram had evidence that could prove America, the New World, belonged to Queen Elizabeth by right of a blood-line that stretched back to the mysterious Prince Madoc.

Ingram's story was strange. For a year he and two other cast-aways had wandered across North America, from Florida to Newfoundland, and seen and heard things that defied the imagination: weird creatures and phenomenal geography. But what really grabbed Peckham was that in his travels Ingram had encountered people who appeared to speak a corrupted and bastardized Welsh. That wasn't really Peckham's field of expertise, but he knew it was John Dee's, so he packed Ingram off to Mortlake in the company of Mr Clement to see what the good doctor could make of the story. If there was any substance to it, both Peckham and Dee were convinced the glory, the destiny anyway, of the Kingdom of England rested on it.

## Cape Breton

In the autumn of 1569 the *Gargaryne*, a French trader, was moored off Cape Breton in present day Nova Scotia when its captain M. Champaign was alerted to a commotion outside.[2] Three English men sitting in a native canoe were calling up, asking to be let on board. Their names were David Ingram, Richard Brown, and Richard Twyde and they told him a story that began in Mexico the year before.

In September 1568, they'd been involved in the battle of San Juan de Ulúa (present day Vera Cruz), when John Hawkins and Francis Drake's small flotilla of five ships was attacked by thirteen Spanish ships under Francisco Luján. Hawkins and Drake weren't just outnumbered but out-thought. After his ship, *The Minion*, was damaged, Hawkins sailed across the Gulf of Mexico where he put 114 of his crew on shore.

European settlements along the Atlantic coast were sparse and some of the men decided to walk back to San Juan, while others including Ingram, Brown and Twyde intended to follow the coast north in search of any people friendly to the English. After some in that group were killed and others returned south, the three remaining sailors had wandered across North America

---

[2] For consistency, the spelling in the original document is used throughout unless it is so obscure the modern is necessary.

until they reached the fishing village at Cape Breton, unintentionally becoming the first Europeans to cross North America.

There are two ways to approach the story of Ingram and his shipmates' journey. If you believe the account that Sir George Peckham recorded years later then it tells an odd and obscure story in the early history of North American colonization. If you have doubts, it becomes the beginning of another that is even stranger in the ways it invokes the visions of empire in Elizabethan England and how they played out in North America.

Ingram existed. Several people independently stated they met him, and they had no reason to make that up, but we know little else about the man save he was born in Barking, these days almost inner East London, back then a fishing village on the Thames. Most Barking lads grew up to become fishermen, which led some, like Ingram, into the Navy, which kept a nodding obedience to the law, and total fealty to the King or Queen.

He was most likely in his mid-twenties when he began his adventure, this assuming he began young with the fishing boats at Barking and worked his way through the ranks learning to use knots, swords and guns. Physically, he was on the short side, yet as a sailor he would have hauled and lifted and been stronger than taller men who weren't used to labour. Chances are he had broken a limb, but he would have been expected to get out of hospital quickly and to do so while the pain subsided, though his arm or leg would never have been the same again. On shore, at home or whenever he could afford to, he drank beer and wine, probably to excess, but then there were long stretches at sea where he had no choice but to be sober. He ate a monotonous diet that provided calories but nothing in the way of taste or variety. He was, or had been, diseased. Syphilis was about; not in the plague proportions it would later be, though sailors and soldiers were prime targets. Smallpox was a more common danger, and bubonic plague, sweating sickness, scrofula, TB and other misunderstood diseases were always threatening to erupt across the society. One, several, possibly all of these experiences had marked him. His skin was crusty, his eyes rheumy, but so was everyone's in Elizabethan England.

He was illiterate. When he later gave his story to Peckham, he didn't write it down but answered Peckham's questions, all of which had a specific purpose Ingram may not have been aware of. He was religious; very likely Protestant, and in the mid-sixteenth century this meant that his contacts with indigenous people were filtered through a mindset that denied their belief systems while his own was wracked with peculiar superstitions.

Compared to many Elizabethans he was also widely travelled. He would have seen the Atlantic coasts of Europe and the Mediterranean, and the African and American coasts. But if his ship anchored in the harbour at Constantinople this didn't mean he disembarked and went into the city. International negotiations were delicate, and it was often safer to keep the crew on board. He only experienced some places from a distance, and he had very little to compare what he saw in North America to what he'd seen elsewhere, which helps explain some of his more fantastic claims.

# Florida

Drake and Hawkins' five ships were moored in the harbour of San Juan de Ulúa when Luján attacked, by surprise according to some reports though given Drake and Hawkins were privateers and slavers they could hardly have complained that was unfair. His ship badly damaged, Hawkins retreated across the Gulf of Mexico before running aground at a point on the west coast of present-day Florida and ordering the crew off. This was where Ingram's account began, or more accurately, the account that he gave nearly twenty years later to Peckham and Queen Elizabeth's secretary Francis Walsingham.

Both men were heavily invested in the case for England colonizing North America. As such they were interested in the physical descriptions, the topography, the people and the flora and fauna that Ingram encountered. The emotional experiences of three sailors entering a world no Europeans had before them were irrelevant.

At least two accounts of David Ingram's journey were circulating among a small group in 1582. Humphrey Gilbert interviewed Ingram from August into September, but he was clearly working from the earlier version and essentially wanted some statements confirmed. He took what he needed and cleaned it up, removing the more feverish claims.

The sections quoted are from the first, the rough, strange version, which survived to become the opening chapter to *Documents Connected with the History of South Carolina*, published in 1856. It is written in the third person, evidence that it was an interview, and scattered throughout are references to people and to plants that Ingram couldn't have identified without help, though Dee would have got their significance immediately. That's a reminder that while we might be reading Ingram, we are really listening to Peckham or Walsingham, their motives and interests and way of thinking. Once Ingram and his two friends are introduced their presence is low key. They are observers, not participants.

We pick it up a couple of paragraphs in, after Ingram, Brown and Twyde have been introduced and the circumstances under which they found themselves in Florida explained.

> The first kings that they came before dwelte in a countrye called Gizicka who caused them to be stripped naked and woundering greatlie at the whiteness of their skin let them dparte (without) further harm.

In 1539 Hernando de Soto had explored the Florida region and encountered people living on the Withlacoochee River he called Guazoco. If these were the same people Ingram met, then contact with Europeans had taken place within living memory. On the one hand, they ought not to have been surprised at the whiteness of the Europeans' skin, on the other, that might not have been why they stripped them naked. Ingram was no cultural anthropologist; Walsingham and Peckham even less so. Nevertheless, the statement gives us a location and a germ of credibility to Ingram's story.

But only a germ. It's curious that Ingram could be vague about so many details yet remember the name of a group of people he spent a few days with more than a decade earlier. Copies of de Soto's account had been floating about since the 1560s, and if Walsingham and Peckham were not fluent in

Spanish, they had no problem finding someone to translate it. Not so long ago, Queen Mary's husband Philip II of Spain couldn't speak a word of English, so all official documents had been produced in bilingual versions. It's a reminder that everything Ingram was to say from hereon would be filtered by two people who knew exactly what others wanted to hear.

The term kings, which is shorthand for kingdoms, was deliberate on Ingram's part. In his travels through the southeast especially, he repeatedly refers to the wealth of the people and the cities they inhabit. The Gizicka typically wear *rubyes, beinge sixe inches longe and twoe inches broade.* The rulers are carried about in a sumptuous *Chayer* (chair) of *Sylver* or *Christall.*

A constant problem with his account is that the credible and the fantastic often inhabit the same sentence. A crystal sedan chair sounds like something out of a fairytale but because copper, silver and gold were worked in pre-Columbian America this statement needs only a slight shift in perspective to be plausible. It is less clear what he meant by rubies, especially of that size. Coral, maybe, though just as credibly, Walsingham and Peckham both knew that the way to pique interest in new colonies was to suggest there were chest loads of fabulous wealth over there, all watched over by people with little concern for protecting it.

More important is his constant reference to cities, a term that in the sixteenth century equated with permanent structures and advanced technologies.

Midway through the account, Ingram says he and his companions seldom stayed anywhere more than three nights. An exception was the city of Balma, "a ritche cyttie a mile and a half long" where they stopped about a week. Other cities he named were Ochala, *a greate towne a mile longe, Bega, a Countrye and a Towne of that name, three quarters of a myle longe, and Gunda;*

> A small towne and a ryver boathe of that name, and this is the most northerlie pte that this Ex was att. They have in every house scoupes, buckettes and dyvers other vesselles of massive sylver.

Fifty years earlier, Francisco de Orellana had entered the Amazon via the Andes and described crowded cities along the banks. By the time the Spanish returned in the 1630s, the cities had disappeared, and the jungle reclaimed the land. That led scholars to assume de Orellana had invented the cities. Much later, archaeologists discovered the footprints of buildings and roads, realizing that before the Spanish re-entered the jungle, smallpox and influenza had already decimated the populations and destroyed the cultures. Before the apocalypse, the cities hadn't just existed, they had developed a trade and communication network that extended into the midwest below Canada, to cities like Cahokia that was once one of the largest in the world.

Something similar happened to the cities that Ingram, Twyde and Brown visited. It would be a century or more before colonists returned to the midwest, by which time the cultures had already collapsed and the cities along the rivers had vanished.

That the three sailors stopped overnight at towns and settlements along the way might look as though they had freedom of movement, but more likely they were traded.

The reasons for thinking this are based on logic more than evidence, but it's hard to believe the three could walk freely from Florida to Nova Scotia without having the protection being precious goods gave them. Ingram didn't have a lot to say about how the inhabitants treated them, but he talks about new plants as food and medicinal sources, and they weren't discovered by chance.

Also, if their journey was unhindered the route, they took doesn't make sense, meandering from the coast into the midwest, roughly northwards to places unknown. By 1569 European ships were sailing along the east coast of America frequently enough that, left to their own devices, the three sailors would have stuck to the shoreline, knowing that was their best chance of being rescued. But that assumes they were allowed to travel freely.

In the 1520s the Spanish conquistador Álvar Núñez Cabeza de Vaca had found himself in a similar predicament, having lost most of his comrades, he and three others had wandered through present day Texas to California and northern Mexico. Gradually, Cabeza de Vaca understood that he was being traded, but that was also the reason he survived, so he acquiesced. Cabeza de Vaca's account was a very different thing to Ingram's, infused with a Catholic spiritualism that saw him believe he was a miracle worker among people who were pagan yet could be saved.

Ingram doesn't say there was any tension with any communities, but then the sailors didn't understand the languages or customs, so transactions could be carried out under their noses without them being aware. And neither Ingram nor Cabeza de Vaca understood the First Nations idea of trade; no-one in Europe really would until twentieth century anthropologists looked into it. In the West, trade was an economic transaction, where ideally the trader came off better than before. For the inhabitants of the New World, it was also a way to keep communications open and maintain civil harmony, with social codes that rendered material value ephemeral.

> If you will bargayne for ware with them leave the thinge that you will sell uppon the grounde, and goe from it a pretye waye of, then will they come and take it, and sett downe suche wares as they will give for it, in the place, and if you thincke it not sufficyent, leave the wares with signes that you like it not, and they will bringe more until ether they or you be satysfyed or will give noe more, otherwayes you maye hange yor wares uppon a long poles ende and so put more or less on it untill they have agreed on the bargayne.

Ignorance was Ingram's greatest asset. Thrown into a culture with only a tenuous resemblance to his, it paid to watch but not analyse too closely. Resemblances after all were not reflections.

> …they doe honor for there god a devell (which) they call Collochio, who speakethe unto them sometimes in the liknes of a blacke dogge, and sometimes in the liknes of a blacke calfe. And some doe honor the sonne, the mone and the stares…he and his twoe fellowes…wente into a poore man's house and there they did see the saide Collochio, or devell (with) very great eyes like a blacke calfe. Upon the sighte therof, Browne said "There is the Devell!" and theruppon he blessed him selfe, In the name of the Father and of the Sonne and of the Holy Ghoste and Twide saide verye vehementlie, 'I defye thee and all thy works!' and presently the Collochio shranke awaye in a stealinge manner, furth of all the doors, and was sene noe more unto them.

In the 1830s George Catlin painted the Mandan, Pawnee and other people living along the Missouri River in present day Missouri and North Dakota. In some of his paintings, dancers are wearing buffalo heads. It doesn't take a great leap of imagination to see the three sailors, who came from a world where Lucifer wandered the earth playing havoc with peoples' lives, witnessing a religious ceremony and thinking the performers were dressed as devils. How the man in the mask would react may be a matter of debate though given the sailors' overheated reactions it would have been prudent to leave them alone.

Whose story this is, however, is always an open question. Sometimes it is Ingram's, and sometimes he is telling Walsingham and Peckham what they want to hear, but often he says things Walsingham or Peckham couldn't have anticipated.

> The people comonlye are of good favor, feture and shape of bodye, of growthe about five foote highe, somwhat thicke, with there faces and skynnes of colloure like an ollive and towarde the northe somwhat tawnye, but some of them are paynted with dyvers colloures, they are very swyffte of foote, the heare of there heades is shaven in sundrye places and the reste of their heddes is traced.

The standard history of first contact between Europeans and the Pawnee and Mandan people begins with the arrival of Jesuit priests in the 1730s. Before then there were no official records of encounter, so Ingram's descriptions including head shaving and tattooing (Ingram's 'tracing') are not only the earliest, but these are details Walsingham and Peckham wouldn't have known about. And they wouldn't have even imagined something so specific, so recognizably human yet foreign as this:

If any of them doe holde upp boathe there handes at lengthe and kisse the backes of them on boathe sides, then you maye undowbtedly truste them, for it is the greateste token of frendshippe that maye be.

By the time Ingram, Brown and Twyde were walking through the midwest, there had been over a century of sporadic contact between Europeans and Native Americans, leaving out the Vikings, whose records of settlement at places like L'Anse aux Meadows five hundred years earlier were lost or forgotten. There was no astonishment in the curiosity that Walsingham, Peckham then Dee had about the inhabitants, and none of the philosophical doubts Spanish monks had regarding their humanity. All Walsingham and Peckham cared about was whether they could do business with them, and, more importantly, what did the inhabitants have to sell?

They have (short) broade swordes of blacke Iron of the lengthe of a yarde or very neare an ell bearinge edges thicker than the backes of our knives.

And:

There are alsoe great Rivars at the heades wherof (we) did fynde sundrye peeces of goulde some as bigge as a mans fyste.

So a lot, apparently. Nobody in North or South America smelted iron, though Ingram could have mistaken obsidian spear and arrow heads for metal, but that story about gold nuggets the size of a man's fist lying about had a pedigree going back to before Columbus's voyages, when there were stories of islands out in the Atlantic where the people led perfect lives, in harmony with work, community, writing poetry and talking to birds. Money and gold were always in abundance. Anybody returning from the New World was expected to bring a report of something fabulous that either they had seen for themselves or had heard about from very reliable sources. Tales about fountains of youth and glittering cities in the Mexican deserts were standard.

Ingram wasn't lying; he was telling his listeners what he thought they wanted to hear.

Collochio hurrying off, slightly embarrassed by the sounds of things, and the Guazoco ordering the sailors to strip naked: these are the only reactions Ingram described the inhabitants' having to the three sailors, and they aren't revelations so much as glimpses. For Peckham especially, the inhabitants' mindsets were irrelevant. Maybe John Dee did interrogate Ingram about how the inhabitants treated him; he had his reasons, but if everything else about how the inhabitants regarded the sailors is conjecture, some theories are stronger than others.

In this land, goods were traded along a web of networks that stretched from Aztec Mexico to the Iroquois in the north, and objects always carried communications with them. By the time the three sailors were cast off the *Minion*, those inhabitants who hadn't encountered Europeans already knew about them. De Soto, Álvarez de Piñeda, Juan Ponce de León, Francisco Vázquez de Coronado, Cabeza de Vaca: they'd all been through the territory, sometimes like Cabeza de Vaca, hapless and at the mercy of the inhabitants, more often with battalions of soldiers in tow. Coronado appeared in the desert with four hundred soldiers and three thousand mercenaries and laid waste in what he called conflicts but were massacres. At one pueblo he ordered dozens of men tied to stakes and burned them alive. He was chasing stories there were cities of gold out in the desert.

These conquistadors were driven by something too deep-seated to be fear, too tangible to be paranoia. This New World was a kind of hell, that looked just enough like the land they'd left to persuade them they could comprehend it, until they reached that moment they lost all reason.

The three sailors were not godlike or even marvellous. Their very ordinariness was something to hold in contempt.

*

The grounde and Countrye is moste exelent fertill and pleasunte, of the Soyls and especyallie towardes the River of Maii, for the grasse of the rest is not so grene (green) as it is in those partes, for the other is brent (burnt) awaye with the heate of the sonne, And as all the countrye is good and most delycate havinge greate playnes as large and as fayer (fair) in many places as maye be sene (seen), beinge as playne as a boarde.

Once they left the damp and enervating swamps on the coast, the sailors found themselves in a landscape that was vaguely familiar, passably England in so far as the view stretching in all directions was of low, green, rolling hills broken up with forest. But this wasn't Ingram talking, it was Peckham, who understood he needed to take what Ingram saw and turn that into what others wanted to hear.

(There is) alsoe great abundaunce of those trees which carrye a thicke barke that bytethe like pep (pepper), of which(kind) younge Mr Wynter broughte home from the

Streight of Magillane with the fruitffull Palme tree and great plentye of other sweete trees (so far) unknowen.

In 1577 John Wynter had been captain of the *Elizabeth*, sailing with Francis Drake on his circumnavigation of the globe. At Tierra del Fuego, he had gone ashore and learned from the inhabitants that they used the bark of canelo trees as a medicine. He collected specimens of the bark and fed some to his crew while keeping the rest in store for home. Tea from Winter's bark, as the tree became known in England, was one of the more sensible preventatives against scurvy.

Ingram can't have known about Wynter, Peckham certainly did, and so too Dee, who understood the references. There was timber in the New World, which the budding empire was going to need to build its ships, but there were also medicines and herbs out there, some sure to cure that riddled menagerie of Elizabethan diseases.

David Ingram's story had been taken up by other voices, none in tune nor with much sympathy for him but like lawyers, hammering it into the shape that each wanted. Not lies or distortions so much as entreaties to anyone listening to see their reasoning. On one subject, however, they had to step back and give him his voice back. It wasn't that what he said was so utterly strange, but they couldn't possibly contradict him.

## The Plains

As the three sailors entered the midwest, the world took on a magical quality.

And after that Playnes againe and in other places great closes environed (enclosed) with moste delicate trees insteade of Hedges, they beinge as it were (built) by the handes of men. Yet the best grass for the moste parte is in the high Countryes somewhat far from the Seasyde and great rivers, by reason that the lowe growndes there be so rancke, (Fertile? Foul smelling?) that the grass growethe faster than it canne be eaten …

Somewhere to the west of the Appalachians, the inhabitants farmed crops, and in the summer, they took their sheep up to the foothills to graze. They grew corn: *a kynde of grayne the eare wherof is as bigge as a mans wriste,* And they lived in cities.

Even so, this wasn't their idea of a *tamed* land. The inhabitants had put down roads and tracks across the plains, but the sailors didn't have to travel far to be out in nature. Down at the coast they had seen flamingoes, which were good to eat.

They see a lot of bison: *in lengthe almost twentye foote havinge longe eares like a bludde hownde, with long heares aboute there eares, there homes be Crooked like Rames hornes, ther eyes blacke.* They notice deer, wild and domestic sheep, goats, hares, rabbits, wolves and cattle. He also see coyotes that he mistakes for foxes (their skins are more grizzled than the ones in England), and then he sees things he shouldn't.

Wild horses for one. Officially, De Soto brought horses into America in 1539, only thirty years earlier. It's difficult to believe they would spread so quickly without De Soto losing them at a careless rate, and unlike coyotes, horses are hard to mistake. So, when First Nations people today claim they had horses before the Spanish brought them, Ingram is on their side.

He saw a giant condor:

There is alsoe a very straunge Birde thrice as bigge as an Eagle, very bewtyfull to behoulde, his feathers are more oryente (Oriental? Exotic?) then a Peacockes feathers, his eyes are as glistering as any Hawkes eyes, but as great as a mans eyes, his heade and thighe as bigge as a mans heade and thighe. It hath a Creste or tufte of feathers of sundrye colloures on the toppe of the heade like a lapwinge, hanginge backwardes. his beak and Tallentes in proportion like unto an Eagle, but very huge and lardge.

The description is more exotic than a condor deserves, with its wrinkled hide and a face even its mother would hesitate to love, though Ingram would hardly be the first to recall some creature as bigger and more brilliant than first impressions allowed. Most animals are familiar enough and the ones he gets wrong make sense. If he confuses foxes and coyotes, his interrogators can follow what he is talking about, but there are moments ruthless pragmatists like Walsingham and Peckham must have wondered what they'd got themselves into.

A Monstruous Beast twyce as bigge as a Horse and in every proportyon like unto a Horse Beast bothe in mayne, hoofe, heare, and neighinge, savinge it was small towardes the hinder ptes like a Greyhounde: these Beastes have two teethe or hornes of a foote longe growinge streight furthe (forth from their) nostrelles, they are naturall Enimyes to the horse.

Albrecht Durer's 1515 woodcut of a rhinoceros vaguely resembles that, and Ingram could have seen a real one if he had visited a North African port, but it sounds more like one of those composite creatures that appeared on maps at the time to fill in the blank spaces, part fish part pig.

The next two paragraphs lifted it from the strange to the weird.

> He did alsoe see in that Countrye boath Eliphantes and ounces.

He didn't. He saw ounces, or cougars or lynxes, but he didn't see elephants.

> He did alsoe see one other strange Beaste bigger than a Beare. It had nether heade nor necke, his eyes and mouthe weare in his Breaste. This Beaste is verye ouglie to beholde and Cowardlie of kynde, it bearethe a very fyne skynne like a Ratte, full of sylver heare.

It is a grizzly, bigger than a bear because the grizzly was bigger than the brown and black bears Ingram had encountered in his world travels, and perhaps with weak eyesight you could think a grizzly had its head in its breast. As for the fur, he must have seen people wearing capes or hats, so were Peckham and Walsingham sniffing out potential investors for the fur trade, offering a cowardly giant mink as bait? Maybe, but still sounds like it came from Ingram, who had his own reasons, including the possibility that he did see what he claimed, even if the circumstances were extenuating. There'd be a lot of them along the way.

At his best he describes the world around him lucidly, with the curiosity of someone aware of how different it is from home. He *hath sene it lighten and thunder in somer season by the space of 24 howres together. the cause wherof he iudgethe to be the heate of the Clymate.* He gives the first description of Midwest tornadoes: *a Clowde somtyme of the yeare sene in the Ayer well comonlye turnethe to great tempestes.* Close to Cape Breton he sees a great auk, it will change his life, but more on that later.

The three men continue northwards, always in the presence of the inhabitants, who remain their guides, protectors and owners. One day on the coast they meet inhabitants who draw pictures of ships in the sand and Ingram realizes that Europeans are not far away. Soon after, others tell him a Christian ship has anchored at the head of a river. The three are taken to the estuary, put into a canoe and sent across, to meet Captain Champlain.

This is the end of their adventure. Their story however is about to take on a life of its own.

## Mortlake II

John Dee House at 9-16 Mortlake High Street is an apartment block. Nothing remains of his actual house, or any of Tudor-era Mortlake except a nearby church tower, but that's to be expected. In 1582, Mortlake was a small village of thatched cottages, removed from London and its crowded streets, noise and disease. John Dee's house sat by the Thames, and some-times Queen Elizabeth would be taken up by barge to receive his astrological readings and general political advice. He had asked the stars for the best date for her coronation in 1558, and so far, the answer had been a good one.

All the pictures of Dees workspace were executed years after he'd died and invariably, they show a library lined with shelves of neatly stacked books, a globe perhaps and a star chart; the scholar as country gentleman. Unsteady towers of manuscripts piled across the table more likely, and maps and charts, some of them pinned to the walls and covered in curious glyphs, jars full of pallid, translucent stuff tinged with mould, or flakes of blue and green metal, dried flowers, inexplicable liquids, and on other shelves mortar and pestles, beakers, funnels and copper discs over candles, the dim, dust choked room humming with chemical odours absorbed into the walls over decades of experiments. The chaos of an ordered mind.

The antiquarian John Aubrey wrote about him in *Brief Lives*. His great-grandfather was a close friend of Dee's and Aubrey's grandmother used to see them wandering along the river. Aubrey heard from others the two friends would go to Dee's house and make concoctions using eggshells, menstrual blood, hair, leather, excrement and other readily available material. He also heard that Dee spent years studying the weather and was so accurate with his predictions some people, like Aubrey's grandmother, were convinced Dee consorted with the Devil.

Dee had been dead sixty-three years when Aubrey made a pilgrimage out to Mortlake in 1672 to see what he could dig up about him. Dee's house was long gone, and he'd disappeared from the records. People weren't even sure where he was buried. The only person in the village who could remember him was old Goody Faldo and, like Aubrey's grandmother, she used to think Dee was in league with dark powers.

But Aubrey perceived a softly spoken man, with a long, snowy white beard over a black gown, his arms hidden under flowing sleeves. Men who saw no political threat from Dee always spoke of him as kindly and gentle, and Aubrey thought that if he'd been a boy back them, he wouldn't have been scared of Dee.

In September 1582 Dee persuaded Sir John Killigrew, a notoriously violent politician, to compromise and settle with some Spanish merchants accusing him of theft. It was so much more sensible than succumbing to vanity and threatening bloodshed. But Dee had more important problems to deal with than a foul-tempered M.P. His wife Jane was ill, complaining of cramps and vomiting bile. In October she fainted at church. Meanwhile a spirit named Lundrumguffa was attacking his newborn daughter Katharin, and he was being pestered by a man named Edward Kelley. At least his research into the language of the angels was progressing. He had already transcribed several conversations:

> 'Are you one of them?' said I, John Dee, "that are answerable (upon due observations performed) to this Stone?'
>
> URIEL: 'I am.'
>
> Dee: 'Are there any more beside you?'
>
> URIEL:'Michael and Raphael. But Michael is the leader in our works.'
>
> Dee: 'Is my Book of Soyga of any excellency?'
>
> URIEL: 'That book was revealed to Adam in Paradise by the good angels of God.'
>
> Dee: 'Will you give me any instructions, how I may read those tables of Soyga?'
>
> URIEL: 'I can. but only Michael can interpret that book.'

Wherever the conversations with angels took him, like all Elizabethan natural philosophers, Dee believed that the universe was built on systems that were logical and rational. If he didn't understand how they worked it was only a matter of cracking the code, so the divinations that came out of astrology weren't random but based on careful, precision plotting of the movement of planets and constellations, and the scribblings in the margins of his consultations weren't so wildly different and every bit as serious as those a mathematician would use to break down an equation.

Which was why people like Queen Elizabeth and George Peckham consulted Dee; they trusted him.

Peckham had no time for angels. He was a pragmatic and hard-headed merchant who dealt with empirical data, also he was Catholic and thought of the supernatural as existing somewhere between fraud and heresy. But underlying his plan for an expedition to the New World was a scheme to put an end to persecution of Catholics by resettling them over there. To propose that to Elizabeth's court he needed an argument that was reasoned and based on evidence, rather than speculation. Dee had already argued for a British empire; one that could be established by right instead of conquest. On the surface his theory was every bit as wild as his conversations with angels, but it was also based on a very specific reading of history.

Dee's obsession with the systems underlying universal laws extended into genealogy, which in Elizabethan England and across Europe was a tool for establishing royal bloodlines and other, vaguer but no less crucial rights of inheritance. Elizabeth was the granddaughter of Henry VII, who had been born at

Pembroke Castle, which identified him as Welsh. The best-known Welsh king was Arthur, and it took some research but Dee could draw a line from Elizabeth back to Arthur, who himself, in Geoffrey of Monmouth's *The History of the Kings of Britain*, could be traced back to Brutus, son of Aeneas of Troy and the founder of Britain. Dee wasn't the only one in Tudor London placing faith in Geoffrey of Monmouth: Shakespeare based King Lear on Geoffrey's Leir and his three daughters, Goneril, Regan and Cordelia.

Geoffrey of Monmouth finished *The History of the Kings of Britain* in the 1130s. A generation later, Owain was king of Gwynedd in North Wales. In 1170 he died and, as was the custom, his sons turned on each other in a war for the throne. One of them, Madoc, tired of the killing, loaded his ship with one hundred and twenty colonists and sailed west. After a few years he returned, looking for more immigrants willing to settle in a land free from want and war. The second expedition departed and was never seen or heard from again.

It sounds suspiciously like the voyage of Saint Brendan, like so many medieval stories where a crisis at home led an adventurer to escape out into the ocean. In time, the adventurer returned with news of a land free from the trouble he'd fled from. If it was famine he found food, if it was war he found an island of peace loving poets, if Muslims invaded he found a community of Christian ascetics practising the true faith in its original and pure form. The point was never that these places existed but there was an inevitability to the original problem that lay in vanity, greed and other human failings. Dealing with them always took the levels of vigour and will that only explorers appeared to possess. Unlike Brendan and the others who came back with news of fantastic lands, Madoc never returned because he had found what he was looking for.

The earliest text with Madoc's story that that we know of that Dee could have read was Humphrey Llwyd's *Cronica Walliae* (Chronicle of the Welsh), written only in 1559, recently so far as Dee was concerned. Madoc rated a paragraph, and Humphrey made clear he borrowed from folklore as much as more respectable sources, so the basic story was floating around, but fact or fable was irrelevant to Dee. The message was clear. If Elizabeth could trace her bloodline back through Welsh kings and a Welsh prince had founded a colony in North America, then she had a legal claim to the continent.

All that so far sounds academic, but the Spanish, the Portuguese and the French were moving in on the New World. As George Peckham would put it in his 1583 pamphlet, *A True Report of the late Discovery and Possession, taken in the Right of the Crowne of Englande, of the Newfound Landes,* the Government needed to act fast to: *restore her to her Highnesse auncient right and interest in those Countries, into the which a noble and worthy personage, lyneally descended from the blood royall, borne in Wales, named Madocke ap Owen Gwyneth.*

John Dee prided himself on his rigour, on his fidelity to truth, *that noble Empress LADY VERITY,* but when it came to propaganda he was as calculating as one of the Queen's courtiers. If the argument that Elizabeth could claim North America as her inheritance was thin, it was sturdy compared to the Madoc legend. Even the Welsh weren't familiar with that one, but that was no problem. Presumably, if a Welsh prince had sailed across to North America, there should still be evidence, somewhere.

Which was why Peckham and Walsingham sent David Ingram to Dee. This man had been out beyond the frontier. He'd seen things no one else had, and somewhere in that curious interview with its descriptions of demon headed priests and strange monsters, might be just the evidence Dee needed.

No record survives of Dee's meeting with Ingram, but he might not have needed one, being only interested in one small question; where was the evidence the Welsh visited the New World. Also, it wasn't wise to keep too many notes, given the treachery at Elizabeth's court and the mercurial speed with which heroes turned to villains. It didn't take much: a whisper in the right ear was enough, and the Elizabethans weren't inventive when it came to inflicting pain, just sadistic. But the world was more complex than that.

Peckham knew people who wanted him out of the way. One of them by rights should have been Francis Walsingham, who had coldly overseen the execution of a few dozen Catholics already, and he had raised fines for failing to attend Anglican mass from a shilling to twenty pounds, or about five thousand pounds in today's money, but Peckham's scheme to found a Catholic colony wouldn't have got anywhere without Walsingham, and vice versa. Cash was the problem. Humphrey Gilbert, the principal advocate didn't have enough, neither did Peckham, and for Gilbert to succeed he needed Peckham, just as much as Peckham needed him.

Walsingham meanwhile could see several advantages to Peckham's scheme. For all the blood already on his hands, he wanted to avoid the convulsions of violence afflicting France after the Saint Bartholemew's Day massacre ten years earlier, when Catholics had butchered as many as twenty thousand Protestant Huguenots. To the south, Spain was looking for a fight, accusing England of taking sides with the Dutch in their struggle against Spanish rule. War against either country was just a matter of time. Clearing Catholics out of England looked like a good idea.

John Dee wasn't remotely interested in these machinations. It was strictly genealogy for him. What he needed to find were the fragments in Ingram's narrative that he could tie in with the Madoc theory. Peckham had most likely sent Dee a copy of the narrative so there was no reason why the meeting needed to be long, or Ingram repeat everything he'd said. It was more a case of Dee pulling out statements and testing suppositions. One in particular stood out.

It was thirteen years since the three sailors had made their journey. Browne had died at sea about five years ago and Twyde two years later near Manchester, so Ingram was alone, against a man who gave the impression he was listening intently, and he was, but not to Ingram's story so much as his own train of thought.

Among the descriptions of elephants, giant birds and breast-headed monsters, one bird almost slips through, unnoticed.

There is alsoe another kynde of fowle in that Countrye which hauntethe the (rivers) neare unto the islandes, they are of the shape and (size) of a goose, but there wynges are covered with small (yellow) feathers and cannot flye.

You maye dryve them before you like Sheepe, they are
excedinge fatte, and very delicate meate.

The next sentence was exactly what Dee was looking for.

They have white heades, and therfore the Countrye men
call them Penguins.

In Welsh, 'pen' means head and 'gwyn' is white. Dee didn't
need more proof than that.

The great auk belongs to the same tragic company as the
passenger pigeon, the thylacine and the quagga; creatures whose
saving from extinction was within our reach, almost in our time,
but the rescue came too late. Related to the puffin, it was bigger,
at around seventy centimetres. Its small feathers designed for
swimming in arctic seas were also its curse; they made excellent
down for pillows, robes and hats and it was hunted until, in
1844 the last two were killed on Eldey Island off Iceland. Before
then, knowing the bird was in danger, museum expeditions had
gone to Eldey, not to save but to kill and stuff as many as they
could, figuring that taxidermy was more economical than
conservation. Once the great auk was gone, it became yet
another symbol for the destruction human greed wrought.

The pain was there in 1863, when Charles Kingsley wrote
*The Water Babies*, a fable against child labour and for Darwin's
theory of evolution, where Tom the chimney sweep meets a
great auk:

And there he saw the last of the Gairfowl, standing up on
the Allalonestone, all alone. And a very grand old lady she
was, full three feet high, and bolt upright, like some old
Highland chieftainess.

For Kingsley, an Anglican priest, the extinction of the great auk went to the heart of human wickedness.

> Once we were a great nation, and spread over all the Northern Isles. But men shot us so, and knocked us on the head, and took our eggs – why, if you will believe it, they say that on the coast of Labrador the sailors used to lay a plank from the rock on board the thing called their ship, and drive us along the plank by hundreds, till we tumbled down into the ship's waist in heaps; and then, I suppose, they ate us.

For John Dee, the bird's story wasn't so interesting as its name. How could the inhabitants of the New World give a bird a name that not only sounded Welsh but could be translated from it, without some interaction in the past? The question is rhetorical; Dee already knew the answer. David Ingram had met people who spoke a diluted Welsh, the legacy of an encounter four hundred and fifty years earlier, with a prince, a man whose bloodline flowed forward all the way forward to Elizabeth. Logically, historically, even legally, Norumbega and a lot more of the New World was hers.

One man who shared Dee's desire for information about America was Richard Hakluyt, but that was about all they had in common. In time he'd become the best-known advocate for the colonizing of America, and in the process deal a death blow to whatever honour Ingram had, but in 1582 he had just published his first book: *Divers Voyages Touching the Discoverie of America and the Ilands Adjacent unto the Same.* It was too late to include Ingram's account to Peckham and Walsingham, and at the time Hakluyt probably regretted that; Ingram's was exactly the type of narrative he'd been looking for: detailed, informative and new.

Later, Hakluyt would describe how he first became interested in geography, visiting his guardian, a cousin, also named Richard Hakluyt, a barrister the Middle Temple who kept in his office maps and globes and sea charts. The older Richard:

> pointed with his wand to all the known seas, gulfs, bayes, straights, capes, rivers, empires, kingdoms, dukedoms, and territories of each part; with declaration also of their special commodities and particular wants which by the benefit of traffike and intercourse of merchants are plentifully supplied.

The younger Richard was hooked, but the key phrase was *the benefit of traffike and intercourse of merchants.* His cousin wasn't pointing to mysterious and exotic lands so much as economic opportunities. All unknown places held the inarticulate promise of untapped wealth.

And if his eyes didn't water at the prospect of the money an investor stood to make, that's because he saw another opening. The merchants and explorers, the people willing to risk their fortunes, even their lives, to reach these places needed a guide. Hakluyt intended to gather every serious account related to the exploration of America that he could find and publish them as part history, part encyclopaedia. For anyone interested in the New World, the book would be indispensable.

*Divers Voyages* led to his magnum opus, *The Principal Navigations, Voyages, and Discoveries of the English Nations*, in 1589, a history of English travellers and explorers. (The full title could fill a small book in itself.) Dedicated to Francis Walsingham, it was divided into three parts. The first opened with the Empress Helena's journey to Jerusalem, to find a piece of the true cross. It bypassed some important details, she was Greek, not English, and married to Constantine I, not the Welsh king Coel, but given one of the sources was Geoffrey of Monmouth, Hakluyt obviously wasn't too concerned with its authenticity. Then again, Tudor historians weren't interested in facts so much as lessons and if Helena's story said something about the intrepid spirit of the English, then good.

The third book, focusing on America, began with the story of Madoc. From a distance it looks as though Hakluyt fell into a classic trap of mixing fact with fable so freely the reader wouldn't know the difference, but in 1589 Madoc was still crucial to the colonizing project, as Hakluyt clearly understood.

> This land must needs be some part of that Countrey of which the Spanyards affirme themselves to be the first finders since Hannos time. Whereupon it is manifest that that countrey was by Britaines discovered, long before Columbus led any Spanyards thither.

Hanno was a Carthaginian who sailed into the Atlantic in the fifth century BCE, but more to the point, Madoc reached North America long before the Spanish. By the late 1580s the colonization of America had reached a state of urgency. Only the year before, the Spanish Armada had attempted an invasion of England that quickly turned to disaster. It might have spoiled the Spanish taste for a fight, but England still needed to assert some moral authority to colonizing America, and so far, Madoc remained the strongest argument. If Hakluyt hadn't included some mention he could be accused of neglecting, even more dangerously, being in contempt of Elizabeth's inherited rights.

To colonize, England needed to know exactly what America had to offer, what the topography was and who lived there, and as Book III progresses, the fog of legend begins to lift. The reports are more focused on firsthand experience and eyewitness accounts, and if tales of gold and gemstones in abundance prick up the ears of potential investors, they aren't anywhere as useful as solid evidence of mountains and plains, sheep and cattle, timber and furs.

The 1589 edition of *Voyages and Discoveries* is sometimes called a masterpiece (Hakluyt thought it could do with improvement) and a bestseller (no such thing existed in Elizabethan London). In a way, it's better thought of as an object, like a Fabergé egg, precious to hold, full of details inside of inestimable value, and well beyond most people's bank balance. Its value has only increased. More than Shakespeare or Christopher Marlowe or other Elizabethan poets and playwrights, *Voyages and Discoveries* sets out how the Elizabethans perceived the world, just as they are on the verge of sailing out to discover what really lies out there. The fantastic Medieval menagerie of winged beasts with human heads and islands of talking birds is giving way to the tangible and observable, to something closer to what we understand as science.

The 1589 edition also included Ingram's narrative. By the next, the 1598 edition, it was out, Hakluyt deciding it lacked credibility. Why he should cut it while keeping mention of Madoc looks counter-intuitive, but it reveals how fast paced politics at the court were, and how quickly knowledge of the world was unfolding.

Between his meeting with Ingram at Mortlake in 1582 and the publication of the first edition, Dee had spent most of his time in Bohemia with Edward Kelley and their wives, furthering his research into communion with angels. He returned to England in 1589 with his family, broke and embarrassed by Kelley's swindling. Meanwhile his house had been sacked and most of his library stolen. In two years, he would be granted a pension and people would still seek his advice on metaphysical problems, but his days at the centre of Elizabeth's court were over.

By the time the second edition was finished in 1598, cancer had killed Walsingham, Humphrey Gilbert was lost at sea, and within weeks of each other John Hawkins and Francis Drake had succumbed to their illnesses in the West Indies. The men of that generation, the first to advocate for settlement in North America, were now too old and their legacy was dubious. Attempts by the English to found colonies in North America had so far failed, twice at Roanoke Island. At the second attempt the colonists vanished, leaving a mystery for centuries of sleuths to grapple with but at its core it was something guaranteed to happen. The astronomer and cartographer Thomas Harriot, who had sailed over with the first attempt at settlement, reminded his readers that the settlers were mostly city dwellers who knew nothing of farming, and the gold they'd been promised was lying scattered about like rubbish had not materialized. The only route out from Roanoke was into despair.

David Ingram also disappeared, back to Barking and thereafter from the record books.

Once Dee and the investors had Ingram's story he served no useful purpose, but his tragedy was that his journey across North America was both epic and revelatory, at a moment when for men driven to know what waited in the New World these were only an annoyance.

Hakluyt could have looked through his own records, to an account left by Miles Philips, another sailor on the *Minion*. Soon after landing in Florida, the various survivors of the attack at San Juan de Ulúa and the struggle across the Bay of Mexico had chosen their destinies. Philips had headed west with one group and Ingram and fifty-two others had gone north. Philips's story was long and involved being captured by the Spanish, escaping, being recaptured, indentured servitude at a monastery for five years, numerous floggings, learning the art of silk-weaving and eventually returning to England. Years later, Philips and Ingram would meet up and Ingram would tell him that after they split up, his group been attacked by inhabitants. Twenty-five had escaped to catch up with Philips's party while Ingram, Twyde and Brown kept walking north.

The 1598 edition of *Voyages and Discoveries* is the masterpiece, the work that in the future everyone turns to, whether they are merchants pondering the market for furs, or distant historians wanting to know how Elizabethans viewed this vaguely known world. It will tell the story of the English discovery of North America, from distant myth to current news, and it will guarantee that David Ingram's journey will be forgotten.

# Patagonia

Step back for a moment, to August 1578. It is nine years since Ingram, Twyde and Brown returned. Not long after they did, they met up with John Hawkins, who gave them a reward, a decent purse presumably, and that will be the last we hear from of them until Walsingham and Peckham are told there's a man in Barking who once walked through the North American interior from south to north. In August 1578, John Dee travels to Norwich and then to Cheam, neither journey very long, and judging by the detail, not especially important.

At the same time, Francis Drake is battling to pass through the Straits of Magellan at the tip of South America. Like the voyage he made with Hawkins in 1567, which ended so disastrously at San Juan de Ulua, he is not exploring but hunting, for Spanish ships. Queen Elizabeth has commissioned him to raid flotillas and small ports, to be a privateer, a pirate acting on behalf of the Queen, or more precisely, the treasury. The humiliation at San Juan de Ulua notwithstanding, it is a job Drake has carried out with ruthless dedication since then. Now the mission is to round South America and raid Spanish bases and fleets in the Pacific. There is no better man for the job in England.

But so far, the fates are against him. The expedition of five ships left Plymouth on November 15, 1577, and the next day two of them lost masts in a storm. As they reach the Strait, bad weather separates two ships from the fleet. One of the crew is accused of using witchcraft. This isn't an allegation that can be lightly dismissed. People believe there are some who can control the weather, and other phenomena. In a few years Shakespeare will write *The Tempest* about one such man. On August 24, 1578, Saint Bartholemew's Day, Drake lands on an island in the Strait with fresh water and timber:

> We fell with three islands, bearing triangle-wise one from another one of them was very fair and large and of a fruitful soil, upon which, being next unto us and the weather very calm, our General with his gentlemen and certain of his mariners then landed, taking possession thereof in Her Majesty's name, and to her use, and calling the same Elizabeth Island.

It will never be seen by another seafarer again.
But this is not the most remarkable sight for them that day.

> The other two, though they were not so large nor so fair to the eye, yet were they to us exceeding useful, for in them we found great store of strange things, which could not fly at all, nor yet run so fast as that they could escape used with their lives: in body they are less than a goose, and bigger than a mallard, short and thick set together, having no feathers, but instead thereof a certain hard and matted down; their beaks are not much unlike the bills of crows; they lodge and breed upon the land, where, making earths, as the conies (rabbits) do, in the ground, they lay their eggs and bring up their young: in such sort, as Nature may seem to have granted them no small prerogative in swiftness, both to prey upon others, and themselves to escape from any others that seek to seize upon them.

This is the first description of penguins by an English seaman, and indirectly it supports Ingram's story. Drake doesn't refer to the birds by name. He has not travelled as far north as Ingram (Spanish America was his only area of interest) and Ingram was yet to be interviewed by Walsingham or Peckham.

But what do sailors do when confronted by strange creatures in a strange land?

> And such was the infinite resort of these birds to these islands, that in the space of one day we killed no less than 3000...They are a very good and wholesome victual.

And so easy to kill. Penguins had no predators to fear on land and as swift and agile as they were in water, they weren't built to escape the hunters. Still, three thousand would turn out to be a relatively innocuous number. A century later, John Narborough, on another secret mission against the Spanish, entered the Straits of Magellan. *Men may kill ten thousand penguins in less than an hour*, he wrote later. This is the same bird he described as: *standing upright like little children in white aprons in company together.*

In 1776 James Cook's third expedition into the Pacific, in the *Resolution* and the *Discovery*, rounded Africa and on Christmas Day anchored off Kerguelen Island. Cook sent the ship's master and navigator, William Bligh, out to take soundings. He reported back that the islands had no trees, nothing much to speak of but an abundance of birds. The expedition artist, John Webber, drew the massive grey and cheerless cliffs of the island looming over Christmas Harbour. The ships lie anchored to the left. In the foreground a small cluster of gormless penguins stand about while a sailor with a club creeps up to them. If they have any questions regarding what he is doing there, they might look to the two dead birds lying to his side.

There are eighteen surviving species of penguin. The biggest is the emperor and the smallest the little, or fairy, and those in between don't come with any more imaginative names. Despite the slaughter, only the Chatham and the Hunter Island penguins have become extinct in recent centuries. The rest have been protected by isolation. European hunters visited parts of the Southern Ocean every fifty or one hundred years, giving the populations time to replenish.

There was a moment in Western Civilization when it stopped being acceptable to massacre penguins in horrific numbers. It's hard to peg to any other cultural shift; thylacines, northern white rhinos, Barbary lions, Caspian tigers and some five hundred other animals were hunted to extinction in the twentieth century, long after the penguin slaughter had ended. And it can't be connected to that other phenomenon, the evolution of the penguin from strange to cute.

Maybe that began in 1949, in *Frigid Hare*, when Bugs Bunny found himself at the South Pole instead of Miami Beach and obliged to protect a doe-eyed penguin from an Eskimo (not the wildest conflation in Looney Tunes). Anxious to get back to Miami and sunshine, Bugs does his best to shake the penguin off, and it promptly weeps ice cubes. Strong men's hearts melt.

Once the Great Auk became extinct, penguin ceased to be a word for any bird in the northern hemisphere. Penguins bear a passing resemblance to puffins and guillemots, the best known of the surviving auks. They share a common colouring, black on top with white bellies, camouflage against seals in the ocean and predators above, but no one today would confuse them.

The word remains David Ingram's only enduring legacy from his journey across America, for a completely different bird, and it may have been put in his head by someone else.

# CHAPTER 3

## The Lost Dutchman

In 1832 a Lieutenant Nixon travelled overland from India to Singapore then sailed across to Raffles Bay on the northern Australian coast, to the west of Croker Island. Just why he'd go there of all places was the first mystery. James Stirling had tried to establish a colony on the bay in 1827 and its failure was so swift and emphatic the British were scared away for a generation.

The gentleman and his party headed south then cut westwards, *travelling for several days over nothing but barren hills and parching plains...having to dig for water every day*, which was also odd, since they had to have been walking through present day Kakadu National Park, and if that area has too much of anything it is water.

Eventually they climbed a hill, and from the summit looked over a sight for sore English eyes: *plantations, with straight rows of trees, through which a broad sheet of water extended...as far as the eye could see.* And at one spot: *a group of habitations, embosomed in a grove of tall trees like palms.* Small boats glided between the trees and the occupants were busy casting or dragging up nets. *It seemed as if enchantment had brought them into a civilized country.*

As the party descended and walked towards the village, a man appeared on the track, wearing skins tanned and cut in a

European style and a tall cap made of hide and covered with feathers. But the best thing was that his skin was white, and he spoke Dutch, badly to be honest, like someone who'd learnt it at school and since forgotten important grammar rules. He could at least explain to the gentleman that the ancestors of his community had arrived nearly two hundred years earlier and here they'd survived, maybe not prospered but from the top of the hill it looked like they'd made something of their lives. And that was a credit to – what exactly? Their ingenuity? Their resilience? God maybe. Without a priest, book or decent paper they had kept the vestiges of Christian belief and custom alive. They had no church but on Sundays, for example, they put down their tools and rested, like all good seventeenth century Dutch Calvinists.

This story appeared in papers across Britain and Australia over the course of 1834, in January in some places, July or September in others, so obviously useful filler but nothing in need of urgent discussion, and some editors clearly thought it was a hoax.

Not so in Perth, the capital of the Swan River Colony. The colony's leader, James Stirling, the same who failed at Raffles Bay, planned an expedition to travel up the coast and make contact with the lost colony. It would be led by Ensign Robert Dale, who had already led expeditions over the Darling Ranges in search of farming land, and it's all there in official records, until suddenly it isn't, as though someone took a breath and asked for a moment's calm. Was this actually a search for the descendants of a Dutch shipwreck, or a way out of the Swan River Colony's morass of incompetence and despondency? Did this voice of reason then raise a hand and say, "Gentlemen (you know already that in all the discussions no women were present), haven't we been here before?"

Among the disconnected strands and trails that make up the history of early European settlement of Australia, the disappointment new arrivals experienced sometimes gets acknowledged as a side issue, rarely a chapter in itself, but it's the driving force behind a neurotic, compulsive search for the magical in a land where that had been thoroughly exorcised.

> We did not find one garden in the place. All had failed…Am just roasted!!! Thermometer 92 in the shade. The natives had numerous fires round us which made the heat intense. Expected every minute to see them come down on us.

That's Mary Ann Friend writing in 1830, a couple of weeks after arriving at the Swan River Colony. It was formally established six months earlier and it is literally Hell on Earth. Even her description of the inhabitants sounds like creatures from Dante's *Inferno*: *I understand the natives are quite naked with straight hair – they are black but paint their bodies red*; all the more resonant because her curiosity is sincere. Fortunately, she won't stay long (though long enough to leave a record of topographical watercolours) and she does think there is hope for the colony, a thought juxtaposed with the relief that she doesn't have to wait around to see hope become real.

In February 1830 the apocalypse is just beginning and most of the colonists don't have her luxury; they've invested too much or they're soldiers under orders but either way they can't pull out. Yet they are desperate, not to escape but for relief, and any story offering that is worth listening to. George Fletcher Moore wrote in his diary that before he arrived later that year, people believed that if they crossed the escarpment they'd find a huge inland sea, which made absolutely no sense to anyone who'd looked at a map recently.

As Moore will find out, sense doesn't hold much value out here. It rarely does when life is at stake.

But what if there was even, or only, a sliver of truth to the story and shipwrecked Dutch sailors had reached the mainland, survived and now their descendants were scratching out an existence in this desolate landscape? It was possible to believe in this in 1834 because every argument refuting the idea came wrapped in a thick cloud of unknowing. Between 1600 and 1720, at least half a dozen Dutch ships of the VOC (Dutch East India Company) smashed on to reefs, lost masts in storms or ran aground on the Western Australian coast. The basic details: names, dates, rough locations, even court transcripts were on record, but small embellishments and casual interpretations were hard to contradict. Ships disappeared out there, cause and fate unknown. What's more, there were accounts of people landing on the coast, followed by their disappointed search parties, leaving the faintest hope for miracles.

*

In November 1629 Wouter Loos was twenty-four. No images or written descriptions of him survive, which is a problem for those people who like to erect monuments to men on record as achieving historical firsts, though maybe in Wouter's case even they'd make an exception. He was from Maastricht, and a soldier in the Dutch infantry, and if he looked like the average Dutch soldier of the seventeenth century, he was around 170cm tall, with fair to reddish hair hanging over the shoulders and a thin beard. He could easily be mistaken for an Englishman, or a German, or a Breton. Depending on where he had seen action, back home against the Spanish, the French or the English, or in the East Indies against Portuguese or local militias, he'd have scars or internal injuries that he'd have to live with, but nothing too serious; there was no point sending incapacitated soldiers into battle. He could still wield a musket or pike, read maps proficiently and sail a skiff, but the most important skill he'd picked up was to follow orders. That was the one all soldiers were taught would keep them alive.

The trouble with following orders, with being a good soldier, is you quickly become a mere annotation in an inventory absent any distinguishing characteristics, but in the last few months Wouter Loos had slaughtered a family including six children, beaten a woman's head in with an axe, raped several others, drowned two men and generally, *has let himself be used by the Godless.* That last judgment was from Francisco Pelsaert, captain on the *Batavia*.

On June 4, 1629, sailing to Java via the Cape of Good Hope, the *Batavia* hit a reef in an archipelago off Western Australia. Pelsaert knew something about these low, barren islands. Frederick Houtman had sailed past them three years earlier and they were marked on maps as *Abrolhos*, lingua franca on the high seas for 'watch out', from the Portuguese for 'eyes open', which didn't happen this time. A map published by Hessel

Gerritz in 1627 showed a scrawl of recognizable coastline not far away. This vague information offered hope that help could be found over there, and that quickly became a matter of urgency. The next day, with passengers and cargo offloaded, the ship started breaking apart.

After a few days fruitlessly searching islands for fresh water, the captain had to risk the crossing to the mainland, and if he couldn't find water there he'd have no other choice but to steer the longboat to Java. He obviously knew trouble was brewing because he crammed forty-seven passengers on a longboat, including the skipper Ariaen Jacobsz, who had been openly plotting a mutiny with the under-merchant Jeronimus Cornelisz. If Pelsaert was wise to separate the two, his mistake was to pick the wrong man to take on the longboat.

It took about a month to reach Batavia, the Dutch entrepôt on Java (Pelsaert's ship was named after it). The return journey to the archipelago on the *Sardam* took twice as long, which included a week or more searching for the islands. Once Pelsaert found them again he sailed in, disconcerted by the silence. The first survivor he encountered was Wiebbe Hayes, who shouted a warning to stay away. While Pelsaert had been navigating his way north then organizing the rescue, Cornelisz and his gang had murdered over one hundred and twenty-five passengers and crew.

Murder isn't a strong enough word for what had happened. The methods involved attacks with rocks, axes, swords and bare hands, strangulation and drowning, but the hardest details Pelsaert had to get his head around lay in the fine balance between discipline and frenzy that possessed the mutineers.

They methodically followed Cornelisz's orders to kill specific people he decided were an obstruction, but the way witnesses and mutineers described events, the moment the mutineers caught their victims they were overcome by a berserk fury, as though rational and irrational were controlled by an on/off switch.

Pelsaert's investigation of the massacre was thorough and forensic, not because he necessarily was meticulous but because the VOC demanded it. This was a firm that believed in account-ing for every cent; even when he made it to Batavia and reported on the wreck, the VOC wanted to justify expense before fitting out a rescue boat. As he examined and interrogated mutineers and innocents, a picture began to emerge of crewmen and soldiers under the spell of a man whose leadership qualities were nothing more than a frivolous adornment, yet somehow Cornelisz had persuaded good soldiers like Loos to kill without any conscience.

> Wouter Loos...battered in her head at once with an axe or adze, until she died, and he then dragged her into a hole in which the predicant's folk had been dragged. Confesses also that he has been very willing in murdering, and he does not now know how he had wandered so far from God.

The murdered woman's name was Maijken Cardoe. Pelsaert would comprehend the murders, the wanderings from God, as stemming from a fear of death, which goes part way to explain-ing things. Soldiers from a nation in perpetual warfare needed to show they were inured to the fear of death, but few of them would have ever grappled with the possibility of dying so far from the known world. Whatever the various churches had to say about God being omniscient, all knowing and so on, it was forgivable to believe that this was a place his power didn't reach to. Loos had already drowned two men and participated in the killing of the predikant Gijsbert Bastiaens, his wife Maria Schepens, six of their children and their domestic, Wijbrecht Claasz. Maijken Cardoe was number twelve.

When Pelsaert had taken the evidence and surveyed the horror, he built scaffolds from scrap off the *Batavia* and hanged Cornelisz, (he cut his hands off first) along with six other mutineers. Loos should have been among them. Reading his confessions, those of his accomplices and witness accounts from the survivors, it's impossible not to see him as one of the very worst, but maybe after accounting for over one hundred and twenty killed by mutineers and hanging seven mutineers himself, the thought of more death exhausted Pelsaert. Instead, he ordered other mutineers including Loos held prisoner to be taken to Batavia, where the VOC would carry out the executions. Faced with being hanged anyway, Loos begged for a deal. He would rather be marooned on the mainland.

That wasn't letting him off, only offering new odds, in Pelsaert's favour. Vague as the best charts were, they were correct that the mainland was close by; he'd been there. The crossing with his overcrowded longboat hadn't been hard but as the South Land gradually came into view, it materialised into a long, ragged line of steep cliffs, hammered by wind and waves. This coast was marked on maps as Eendrachtsland, the name of Dirk Hartog's ship when he passed through on 1619. Eendracht meant unity, but so far Eendrachtsland was several delicate lines on the map drawn by a shaky hand. The information for those lines had mostly come from men who'd seen the coast from a safe distance. What lay beyond the cliffs was anyone's guess.

Pelsaert did know something the maps couldn't show. The people who lived here kept out of sight. He'd had two encounters on the journey to Java. The first, six crewmen swam to shore to search for fresh water. In the evening light Pelsaert watched four inhabitants creep up but run back as one of the sailors suddenly appeared from behind a rise. Two days later the longboat made another landing and this time they saw eight men gesturing from a safe distance, but when some sailors advanced, they ran off. All Pelsaert could say about these people was they were naked and black, which only supported earlier descriptions. Whether their gestures were warnings wasn't something he could say, but that uncertainty at least left the possibility that if a sailor was stranded here the inhabitants might offer help.

And Loos would be given something else he'd need, a companion.

Jan Pelgrom de Bye was eighteen years old. He had been the cabin boy on the *Batavia*, a good position for a young sailor with ambitions because he'd learned a lot, from cleaning decks to tying knots to steering a small skiff, breaking down and cleaning small guns and clambering through ratlines and up masts to fix the rigging. He'd also worked harder than anyone else on board, being both the Captain's PA, the ship's cleaner and assistant to the crew's cook. Pelsaert liked Pelgrom de Bye; the evidence for that lay in his acute disappointment listening to the cabin boy's testimony, Pelsaert's language achieving a vividness he didn't waste on others. (Pelgrom) *behaved in a godless manner in words and deeds, more fitting to a beast than a man*, and, *a disciple of his master, the Godless seducer and murderer of men, and has followed in his footsteps in murdering, as well as what he still had in mind to do.*

Pelgrom de Bye had killed three people, pleaded to run a sword through a fourth, and raped three women, all the time *mocking at God and cursing and swearing*, yet when he heard the sentence of execution passed, he wept like a child.

That touched Pelsaert, so when Pelgrom de Bye begged through his tears to be left with Loos on the mainland, he agreed.

His mercy was ambiguous. So far as these two were concerned, Pelsaert thought they were *death deserving delinquents* and that fate was not far off. If the two couldn't find a source of fresh water they'd be dead within days, if they did, life might stretch to weeks, depending what food they found. Apart from the ship biscuit and water, a musket, ball and powder were standard kit for marooned sailors, because there always came one despairing moment they'd reach for them.

Pelsaert offered something more generous than a gun, a small dinghy, but even that gesture was double-edged. Weeks earlier, he had sent the skipper of the *Sardam*, Jacob Jacobsz, and four men out in a two masted tender to gather equipment and supplies from the *Batavia* now scattered over the reefs. The next day they were spotted in the distance as a front moved in, minutes later they disappeared into fog. The storms lasted two days, with Pelsaert having no choice but to stare out his cabin window at a blank grey seascape. Once that cleared, he spent days searching for the tender, without luck. So the dinghy was partly a figment of hope for Jacobsz and his crew, on the slim chance they had landed on the coast, and for something else. In his dry, knowing way, Pelsaert wrote in his log that he was marooning Pelgrom de Bye *in order to make himself familiar with the inhabitants of this land and to search out what is happening here.*

In time, his masters at the VOC would hang Pelsaert out to dry for what happened on the archipelago but here he was, the perfect employee. At this moment, The South Land was a blank on the map needing to be filled and if there were more pressing matters requiring his attention, he could at least make the castaways useful. Find out what Eendrachtsland was like and if by chance the two were rescued by a passing ship, this could be their redemption.

Pelsaert even knew where to maroon the two. While searching for Jacobsz and the missing boat, he had been drawn to smoke rising from the mainland. Hoping it was the sailors he'd sailed for the beach and found it empty, save the footprints criss-crossing the sand. These weren't Dutch feet, he knew that much, but if there were people living close by, he could leave Loos and Pelgrom de Bye here and with luck they'd be taken care of.

So the first European occupants on the Australian mainland were dropped off on a beach,[3] at which point they vanished like ghosts. It's possible that local Aboriginal people found and took care of them, so it's also possible they not only survived but flourished, but not likely.

---

[3] Generally agreed to be near the entrance to the Hutt River.

Then as now, the first rule in becoming lost is to remain calm and rational, but these two had just spent weeks in a state of violent hysteria, a kind of panic, and that wasn't going to calm down as soon as they set foot on dry land. They would need the inhabitants' help in order to survive, but the problem was not the response of the people who lived here to them, rather the two sailors to the inhabitants. Communication and negotiation were going to require nuance, something both had cashed in during the days after the *Batavia* wrecked. Maybe the inhabitants brought them water, or maybe they sat in the dunes and watched them die with the casual curiosity we give to injured insects. In any case, though search parties went out to find them, Loos and Pelgrom de Bye were never heard from again.

*

Throughout the seventeenth century Dutch and English ships sailed along the Western Australian coastline, the crews watching it roll past with that blank indifference men give into when they are bored with waiting for whatever they've been promised to show its face. These were merchants and traders; they wanted towns with money so that from out in the ocean they could still see crowded ports, at the very least farms with roads, and nothing that passed by came close to that.

In 1616 Dirk Hartog sailed into this part of the world. It was uncharted, unknown and he was here by accident. Hartog was sailing for Batavia in Indonesia, on a new route. Rather than follow the African coast, to India and Ceylon and then the

Indonesian islands, he was to round the Cape of Good Hope and head due east, across the Indian Ocean, riding the trade winds until he turned north and sailed up to Indonesia. This would cut weeks off the journey. Unfortunately, without being able to measure longitude, that turn off point was guesswork and Hartog overshot it, but the mistake led to him finding some low-lying islands and beyond them a long stretch of coastline. He spent two days mapping the coast and, as previously mentioned, named it Eendrachtsland, after his ship. On an island off Shark Bay now named after him he hammered an inscription on a pewter plate and left it for others to find later, then he sailed north to Bantam.

Three years later Frederick de Houtman sailed into the archipelago where the *Batavia* would later wreck. He wasn't wildly impressed. *This South-land, as far as we could judge, seems to be a very fair coast, but we found it impossible to land on it, nor have we seen any smoke or signs of inhabitants there; but further investigation is wanted on this point.*

His second in command, Jacob Dedel, was a tad more optimistic.

We used our best endeavours to make a landing, which, however, could not conveniently be done owing to the steep coast, whereupon we resolved to run a little more north, where the coast seemed easier of access; but the wind steadily blowing very stiffly from the north under the land, and the tide coming in from the south, we spent a good deal of time in tacking, until a sudden squall from the west, which made the coast a lee-shore and made us lose one of our anchors, threatened to throw us on the coast…We have seen no signs of inhabitants, nor did we always keep near the coast, since it formed large bays which would have taken up much time.

Still, he thought there was hope. *In 27 degrees we came upon the land discovered by the ship* Eendracht, *which land in the said latitude showed as a red, muddy coast, which according to the surmises of some of us might not unlikely prove to be gold-bearing, a point which may be cleared up in time.*

The disappointment was misguided but it wasn't unjustified. Houtman and Dedel had their reasons for expecting more from this place.

Ever since Marco Polo's *Travels* was disseminated in various forms in the fourteenth century, spice traders and merchants had kept in mind that south of China lay lands so rich in pepper, nutmeg, cloves and other spices they could be smelled offshore before the land came into sight.

One was called Java, and: *According to the testimony of good seamen who know it well, this is the biggest island in the world, having a circumference of more than 3,000 miles. The people are idolaters ruled by a powerful monarch and paying no tribute to anyone on earth...It is visited by great numbers of ships and merchants who buy a great range of merchandise, reaping handsome profits and rich returns. The quantity of treasure in the island is beyond all computation.*

Not far away (Marco Polo's distances were always arbitrary) sat another island rich in spices. This was called Lokak: *The people are idolaters, ruled by a powerful monarch and speaking a language of their own. They pay no tribute to anyone, because their country is so situated that no-one can go there to work mischief.*

Lokak, with its spices and elephants and idolaters, became Lucach, or Locach, which eventually appeared on maps, and on one in particular, as Beach (Be-ack).

Houtman had first sailed through Indonesian waters on the First Dutch Expedition to the East Indies in 1595, on the *Hollandia,* as an assistant to Pieter Keyser, whose task was to map the southern constellations in the sky and landmasses below them. The two were following directions from Petrus Plancius, who is the key figure here. Plancius was a cartographer and astronomer at a time when there wasn't a huge difference between the two. In both cases the task was to accumulate observed information and plot it on charts as accurately as possible. That rarified appreciation of geographical and astronomical systems that would distinguish the two came later.

Plancius wasn't on board the *Hollandia,* he never went even close to Indonesia, but he provided Keyser and Houtman with information on the region so detailed it could only have come from first-hand knowledge. He had drawn maps showing routes to the East Indies in 1592 that he provided to a group of Dutch merchants. The VOC didn't exist at this stage, there were small companies competing for access to the sea routes and the information Plancius gave the merchants was the most detailed and recent available. Just where he got it is still a mystery but most of it had to have come from Spanish and Portuguese sources, so he came by it illicitly, involving spies and secret payoffs, or simply theft.[4]

---

[4] Fun fact: Frederick de Houtman happened to be in Lisbon the year Plancius created his maps.

One of his maps was of the East Indies archipelago and at first glance today it is almost right yet completely wrong. Plancius was a modern man, a Protestant fundamentalist and a champion of scientific methodology, which sounds contradictory. but he was driven to smashing Catholic mythologies and replacing them with tangible evidence. This was difficult when dealing with the unknown. Even his hero, Gerardus Mercator, when faced with uncharted regions on his maps of the world, was inclined to invent features like towns and mountain ranges just to avoid blank spaces. That was anathema to Plancius, so, apart from six fish and four ships as decoration,[5] his map of the East Indies contains nothing that hadn't been verified. That isn't the same as being proved accurate; only the western part, the bird's head of Papua New Guinea, appears from the island and it corresponds roughly with our understanding today. Likewise, the shapes of Borneo, Ceram (Seram), Mindanao and other islands need some suspension of disbelief, but Plancius didn't have longitude to correct positions, and their locations are close enough to be recognizable. This information had come from navigators who sailed through the region, and we know that because along the northern coast of New Guinea Plancius indicated safe harbours, which is not something a responsible cartographer would invent.

The map's implicit inaccuracies mean it wouldn't be any use for navigators, but below New Guinea Plancius drew in cuttings of sandalwood, cloves and nutmeg, making the map both a geographical guide and an argument for merchants to send ships

---

5 They also help differentiate land from water for viewers in a hurry.

out. Anyone planning an expedition could glance at the map and grasp the wealth in spices out there and the geographical spaces they would have to contend with. There's no point in promoting myths and legends; in this modern, rational world where mercantilism is emerging as the predominant economic philosophy, verifiable knowledge is the way to power.

In the bottom left-hand corner is a small promontory of Beach. Its jagged outline is general enough to match a few places in northern Australia, the coast above Kalumburu in Western Australia, or Melville Island, even the promontory above Raffles Bay, but if every other detail in the map is a fact (as that word was understood by a sixteenth century geographer aware he had only scraps of information to work with) it isn't there by accident or invention. Somebody sighted and mapped it, and Plancius copied exactly what he had without embellishment; otherwise he wouldn't have included it. While the detail is lacking, only one small river running south, its presence by implication is that the spice trade could extend there, at the least it is worth investigating.

There's no record that the *Hollandia* or the other three ships in the Expedition, the *Amsterdam*, the *Duyfken* and the *Mauritius*, sailed close enough to the Australian mainland to sight Beach[6] but they had their reasons not to. Between leaving Holland and reaching Indonesia, nearly a third of the crew and passengers (71 of 250) died from scurvy. Ships were attacked, some of the officers and crew were captured, it was all the usual

---

[6] Ten years later the *Duyfken* became the first European ship on record to do that when it landed at Cape York Peninsular.

disasters driven by ignorance, naivety and arrogance, and in the end, after various officers had been buried or released from prisons around the islands, the survivors were in a hurry to get back home.

Still, Plancius didn't think the expedition was a total failure. Keyser and Houtman mapped over one hundred and thirty stars, and the voyage of the *Hollandia* became one of those cultural shifts barely noticed as they unfold. Within a few years the mythology and folklore that made earlier maps such wondrous objects would be comprehensively erased from them. The shape of distant lands and how to reach them were much more important.

The exception was Terra Australis, the South Land, which still appeared on the very science based Blaeu map of 1635 as a long coastline circling the southern pole, with one area marked as the Land of the Parrots, on the off chance there was such a place.

So, when Houtman sailed along the coast in 1619, he was hoping that the mystique was still attainable; somewhere north or south there was a land of spices and gems, of colour, not one of insurmountable cliffs, rough seas and inhabited by reclusive, enigmatic people. When he couldn't find what he was looking for he moved on, which is what others following his trail would do. This wasn't the same as denying that there was a place called the Land of Parrots on a promontory called Beach, only that that must be somewhere else.

On Gerritsz's 1627 map, Eendrachtsland jutted into the ocean north of the Abrolhos. To its south lay a small sliver of D'Edelsland, named after Houtman's second in command on the 1619 voyage, and further south was another disconnected line marking Leeuwin, or Lioness, Land. Like Eendrachtsland, it was named after the ship that sailed past in 1622, but who the captain was and how he found himself so far south weren't questions that bothered Gerritsz.[7] Presumably it was a happy accident, like Francois Thijssenn's. Five years after the Leeuwin turned up at the southern tip of Western Australia, the captain of the *Golden Seahorse* sailed further east, tracking cliffs that were even more forbidding and storm battered than Leeuwin Land. Thijssenn named this stretch Nuytsland, after Pieter Nuyts, the highest ranked officer from the VOC on the voyage. It would stretch from east of present-day Albany to just over the border with South Australia. Within a few years of the *Batavia* smashing on to the Abrolhos reefs, the coast was taking shape on European maps in a way that makes it recognizable today.

The convention among European nations – you couldn't call them empires at this stage – was that whoever saw a land first had naming rights, which was the same as giving it an identity. New Spain and later New France and New England were not just claims for ownership but the right for that nation to remake the land in its own image and impose its cultural values upon it.

In the early seventeenth century the standard practice was to honour patrons, royal figures or members of the crew, which might not sound as emphatic as giving a place a nation's name but amounted to the same thing. No one looking at a contemporary map of the South Land, rough and uncertain as it was,

[7] The mystery wasn't solved until 2021, when Nonja Peters and a team of researchers found Jan Fransz's name in Dutch archives.

would miss the detail that the Dutch had been there before other Europeans.

Translated into English, Lioness (Lleeuwin) and Unity (Eendracht) Lands make the South Land exotic and worth further exploration, but anyone interrogating the sailors who'd seen these places would be frustrated by their ignorance. The number who'd made landfall wouldn't have filled a dinghy, and if they had landed on a beach, they hadn't ventured beyond it. The inhabitants stood and gestured from a distance, making their intentions impossible to read, neither hostile nor welcoming though suspiciously unimpressed with the visitors.

Out beyond the reefs and the breakers, Eendrachtsland was a thin, shadowy strip separating sea from sky. If it was mysterious it was not especially enticing, and the names the expeditions gave to those parts they did see were no more than footnotes in a ship's log. The maps were bare of details because the expeditions could not add to them and often had no desire to. As the map began to resolve itself, as the lines extended and De Witt's Land joined Eendrachtsland, which joined Dedel's Land, which had Lleeuwin land to its south and to the east of that, Nuyts land, the growing response was indifference. Closer into shore, sailors struggled against high winds and watched enormous waves pound the cliffs until, exhausted, they backed away.

Every so often expeditions were asked if, on the off chance they happened to be in the area, to see if there was any sign of Loos and Pelgrom de Bye or what had happened to them, but that was a formality. The two castaways were dead; leave them that way.

Unity Land, Lioness Land, maybe some cartographer in Amsterdam looked at recent maps and felt a sudden pang of nostalgia for a time not so far back when the Land of Parrots evoked strange and marvellous places, but this was becoming a culture of hard-headed pragmatists. Colonization being what mattered now, the scrawled lines on the charts told a different story about the South Land. It may have been there was nothing out there worth claiming.

*

The wreck of the *Batavia* carried a clear moral: abandon order and the only course open leads to chaos. The wreck of the *Vergulde Draak* in April 1653, the *Gilt Dragon*, was never so straightforward. It crashed on to a reef with such force that one hundred and eighteen of the one hundred and ninety-three crew and passengers were killed before the survivors could struggle to shore. The good didn't succumb to the wicked but to nature, which has no particular feelings for humanity.

For centuries, the only named voyager on the ship was the skipper Pieter Albertszoon, until in the late twentieth century letters written by the chaplain Hendrick Driessen came to light in VOC archives. The VOC was generally scrupulous with its records but if there was ever a clean-up of paperwork to make space, the names of long vanished sailors could go straight to the incinerators. As with battles, the names of the lost at sea never mattered as much as the numbers.

Albertszoon put seven men on a rowboat and sent them to Batavia to get help. They made it, a phenomenal feat of endurance, but the sixty-eight who remained on shore vanished as silently as a puff of wind.

So did the men who'd soon join them. Two ships, the *Witte Valck* and the *Goede Hoop* were sent out to search for the survivors. Wind and waves prevented the *Witte Valck* from making a landing but three sailors from the *Goede Hoop* did make it to shore. They disappeared from view and then eight more went after them. They also disappeared, though wreckage from their boat was spotted on the shore.

The captain of the *Goede Hoop* gave up at this point; like everyone else he decided that searching for a safe landing was more trouble than it was worth.

By now, eighty-one crew and passengers from Dutch ships had been marooned on Western Australian shores. Maybe the biggest mystery is not what happened to them but how from so many no sign whatsoever would survive.

The *Vergulde Draak* struck the reef off present day Ledge Point, about one hundred kilometres north of Perth. At the northern tip of the Swan coastal plain, more specifically the Quindalup dune system, it is dry, windswept and scrubby, not a place to inspire poets – unless they were looking for analogies with Jesus's temptation in the desert. If the seventeenth century Protestants could agree with Catholics on one thing it was that the desert was a metaphor for Hell, hot and waterless and relentless in its systematic draining of life. The Garden of Eden was lions lying down with lambs by calm, cool rockpools while the desert was crawling with scorpions and serpents, and, even with winter storms brewing as the survivors reached safety, they could have recalled these landscapes in paintings where people had been exiled for unnamed sins.

On Dutch maps, this coast was marked as D'Edel's Land, of which nothing more beyond that scrawled line could be said of it, but people had been living here for more than fifty thousand years. Fresh water wasn't hard to find, if you knew where to look. Had the survivors travelled inland just a short distance they would have hit a river the inhabitants called Garban. Two centuries later George Fletcher Moore, the same who'd doubted the presence of an inland sea, would find it and a soldier on the expedition would call it Moore River in his honour. If the survivors had followed it downstream they would have reached the estuary, which, as every person born by the ocean knew, offered excellent fishing, and here especially in the autumn as schools of tailor, herring and snapper move north to spawn. With just one musket or pistol at hand the survivors could have hunted wallabies, but they'd be better off trapping them, the way they would rabbits back home. Without knowing which plants were safe to eat, going by smell and avoiding berries and fungi would limit suffering to stomach aches and the runs rather than full blown poisoning.

Moore and his team described deep water pools where their horses luxuriated after a day's travel and based on their reports white settlers began moving sheep and cattle into this region. It wasn't great land the way the plains over the escarpment or the hill country much further north would be, but it wasn't bad either. Cattle could wander freely through the scrub and when the time came to round them up they were never far away and, even better, still alive.

Loos and Pelgrom de Bye most likely died quickly, from thirst, hunger or exposure in a matter of days. Up around the Murchison River the heat in early December can be strong enough to take an unready person out in a few hours. Eagles, ravens and dingoes would make short work of their remains and their dematerialization would be complete. They may as well have never set foot on this land, but how sixty-eight people could vanish without trace is baffling.

Not long after George Fletcher Moore found the river, he sat down with Noongar men around the Perth area building up a dictionary of their language. He was different among the colonists in understanding that not only was he a trespasser but it was common sense to try to communicate with the inhabitants on their terms. Unlike Stirling and the other leaders, he was also curious who these people were and where they had come from. One of the stories they told him was that at some point in the past thunder and lightning crackled above the ocean and Rottnest Island became separated from the mainland. Moore didn't realize it, no one would for more than a century, that the men were describing an event that took place about seven thousand years earlier. In a non-writing culture, oral history is the archive and it can survive for centuries without much change to details.

In the storehouses of memory – oral history, rock art, song – the sudden arrival of sixty-eight white-skinned people wearing curious outfits and speaking an unintelligible language should survive in some form. It may have, though first somebody has to ask for it to be revealed, then they have to understand it. Two hundred years later, in 1846, and at the other end of the Earth, the Franklin expedition became trapped in the Arctic and the crew disappeared. The mystery of what happened to them persisted until researchers returned to Inuit oral accounts and realized that the odd behaviour the Inuit had described were consistent with lead poisoning (and that the cannibalism the Inuit claimed to see did happen). Moore's account, which to reiterate, he missed its significance, came out of an interview when he was trying to work out how long the people had been living here. No one asked the local Noongar people what had happened to the survivors of the *Vergulde Draak* until well into the twentieth century, by which time European education had been enforced with corporal punishment and details were missed, then lost, then forgotten.

Even so, sixty-eight people take a lot longer to die than two. With that many to draw on, more of them can be delegated to search for food and water, they can even work in shifts so the sick and weary can rest, and the skill set is broader. There are people who know how to hunt and fish, how to cook, build from raw materials, tend to wounds and illnesses, even how to navigate by the stars should the party want to walk north, on the off chance Batavia was closer than they thought. They should never have disappeared as efficiently as they did.

The advantage in vanishing without trace is that the theories can never be disproved. In the 1920s, station hands reported that at Walga Rock, some three hundred kilometres inland from the coast, the clear depiction of a European sailing ship sat among art in a gallery created by Aboriginal people centuries earlier. For a while the press toyed with the idea that somehow survivors from the *Vergulde Draak* made it this far inland. There weren't many professional experts on cave art to challenge the stories until the 1960s and when they did, they were typically cautious, using words like maybe and possibly, which are the bane of tabloid journalists. It fell to Colin Jack-Hinton from the Western Australian Museum to make the call and he didn't think it was Aboriginal in origin, but he also thought it could be as old as three hundred years, putting it in the time frame for survivors from the wreck.

It says something about how new studies into cave art were that the professionals back then would hesitate to commit because today even someone with a passing interest in the subject would spot the Walga ship immediately as something other than Aboriginal. It looks too much like a western child's idea of a sailing ship. But that puts the blame on the anthropologists and art historians when really it was the journalists, who knew how to recount a mystery while holding readers' attention.

Other propositions put their advocates in the same perilous position. Were there traces of Dutch in the Nhanda language of the Murchison district? Historians thought there was a chance, linguists none at all. What about the genetic disease porphyria found among Aboriginal people from the Murchison but not in other regions? The Netherlands could be one source, but more likely South Africa, which had a small Dutch population in 1652, the year the VOC established trading posts. But if the people of the Murchison had been infected by Dutch sailors, it was likely to happen well after the wreck of the Vergulde Draak, and that points to the biggest problem. People didn't start asking the question until more than one hundred and fifty years of white settlement had passed, by which time the evidence was dilute and hazy. With those same rules, it isn't hard to see how, in 1834, having a few scraps of evidence colonists could, well, not exactly believe in but fearfully hope there was a lost colony further north that could save them.

We all leave a trace. The hand prints Aboriginal people left on Walga Rock are autographs and even if we can't interpret them, they are as valid as a signature on a vellum manuscript. Those material signs are the first thing researchers look for but there are others, cryptic and intangible but every bit as validating. An Aboriginal woman says her blue eyes can be traced back to Dutch survivors from a shipwreck. DNA testing can't establish her claim; it can't differentiate Holland from England, Scotland or France, but it can't prove her wrong either. The trace speaks for itself and no one else.

But it is most effective when it is an anomaly. The gravestones found in China of two fourteenth century Italian children, which we saw in the introduction, may be all that remain of their identities, but they attest to the children living and dying in a place we wouldn't expect to find them. Another trace: the remains of a man uncovered at Amesbury, near Stonehenge, in 2002. He had died and been buried around 2300 BCE, yet archaeologists were able to reconstruct a medical history, including genetic issues and injuries probably from falling from a horse. The grave goods, arrowheads and beakers, indicated he had good social standing, and oxygen isotope analysis of his teeth showed that he had spent his childhood, even been born in what's now Alpine Germany. The image of neolithic people as welded to the village and incurious about what lay over the hill was nonsense. We know so much about that man's life that the word 'prehistoric' is literally redundant. And like the silent stones of the Italian children, he had as much to say about our paucity of imagination as about the nature of society in the past. It's ironic then that we know more about Binot Paulmier de Gonneville, a fictional explorer, than there is about the sixty-eight survivors of the Vergulde Draak.

Of course, they're on record. The need among clerks to record every detail is as ancient as it is compulsive, so somebody was married in a village church, a child died from fever, a sailor got drunk and was sent up before a magistrate, and their names are still in ledgers now locked away in the National Archives in the Hague, though no one today will make the connection without astonishing good fortune and coincidence. So the survivors who reached the shore were doomed to eternal silence, but how could it be any other way?

In 1718 Jean Pierre Purry was in Batavia, working for the VOC and thinking about empires. On maps of the world he could see that the outlines of most of the continents were mostly intact, the interiors might be blank but Britain, France and Spain had carved up North America between themselves. Spain, Portugal and the Netherlands claimed most of South America; Britain, Portugal, the Netherlands and France were dividing up Africa; and Britain, Portugal, the Netherlands and France had moved into Asia. These interiors were inhabited by cultures with cities, writing systems, economies, science, mathematics but that was of no interest to Purry.

What he really wanted was an empire of his own, a patch of land on which to build a colony based on his principles (whatever they were) and a monument to his vision and ideas (also, whatever they were). The first task was to locate it, and while land might be going begging in far northern America or deep in unexplored jungles, he understood that without a sustainable climate he'd have nothing to build his dreams on.

The Spice islands were fertile, jungles literally erupted from their dark soils, but they were also humid and feverish, sapping body and soul. Europeans sent out here spent a considerable amount of their depleted energy trying to get home.

In his travels to Saharan Africa Purry had made the not difficult observation that away from the coast there wasn't a lot of vegetation in view, and not a lot of grains being shipped out. Mediterranean Europe was different, practically anything could grow there. The problem for the Sahara was climate. At the equator the climate was extremely stable, with very little change in temperature, rainfall or hours of sunlight. At the very north and south poles the daily hours of sunlight moved from almost twenty-four hours of sunlight in summer to almost zero in winter. Common for the time, Purry divided the globe into thirty zones of latitude, each thirty degrees, or minutes, wide, so the difference between the Equator and the Poles was twelve hours.

Clearly, for agriculture to thrive, a colony needed to be sited on the best latitude, in the temperate zones north and south of the Equator. That was obvious, Purry didn't need scholars to tell him that, but it wasn't a conclusion, only a start in determining the best site for his colony. The ideal would have four seasons, none extreme, with rainfall in the cooler months and sunshine in the warmer ones. Logically, a temperate climate would produce a mild landscape, with hills rather than mountains, well-watered by rivers slowly making their way to the sea and soil that was not heavily alkaline or acidic, somewhere like Tuscany or Arles.

Finding the equivalent in the rest of the world was going to require data on average temperatures and rainfall, soil types, wind speeds, vegetation types and other details a man couldn't gather in 1718 unless he sailed out to find them. The alternative was to work from a law of averages, so searching an area with a similar parallel to southern France, Purry assumed it had the same climate. He could do that at home, with maps and compasses.

The best lands would be found at the latitude of 33 degrees, where soil fertility, air temperature and hours of sunlight would be most conducive to agriculture. The proof lay in the Mediterranean conditions found from Spain to Syria. By Purry's calculations, the Cape of Good Hope at the tip of Africa was very good, and another was the coast that would turn up in translated copies of his pamphlet as the Land of Nights, Nuyts Land.

> The Land of Nights with its isles, among which I comprehend those of Leeuwin and Edelsland, which is contained in the fifth climate between 30 and 36 deg. of latitude…There is no country in Europe which exceeds it for goodness.

Still, Purry had to anticipate objections. The cost of labour was one, and he couldn't say how willing the inhabitants of Nuyts Land were to work for him, but importing slaves for the new plantations was a simple answer to both of those problems. As for those mysterious inhabitants, kindness and encouraging them to take up the arts and sciences would quickly overcome any hostility. Any other problems would resolve themselves because Nuyts Land had the best climate in the world. The people who immigrated to Purry's new colony would prosper under perfect weather because they were good Calvinists. The term Protestant work ethic didn't exist yet but if Dutch Calvinists were asked what distinguished them from Catholics, or Anglicans, they'd say it was their unwavering subjugation to the rules and their stolid enthusiasm for work. In time an outpost of Europe would emerge on Nuyts Land: Dutch, Protestant, sensible, sober and, thanks to slaves, in want of nothing under the sun.

The VOC didn't buy it. After years of shipwreck, lives lost at sea and a complete failure to find anything of lasting interest, it had already abandoned any idea of colonizing the South Land. If the English and the French were starting to show interest the VOC was of the opinion they could have whatever they found.

The last chance for a Dutch colony had died, not that Purry noticed. If he had got closer to Nuyts Land than a map, Purry would have found a coastline with higher cliffs, rougher seas and wilder storms than anywhere on the South Land that so far had scared off the VOC. Above and behind them lay the Nullabor. If his crew found a beach and managed to climb up the dunes, all they had to look upon was a plain as flat as a blade in every direction. Nothing taller than a clump of sedge as far as they could see.

Eight years after Purry made his proposal, Jonathan Swift also looked at a map. He was writing a satire, *Gulliver's Travels*, and was thinking of somewhere so distant and isolated that readers could accept the unlikeliness of his hero's travels, so he set the land of the Houyhnhnms on one of the islands off the coast of Nuyts Land. The Houyhnhnms are talking horses, their dumb work animals humans called Yahoos. Ultimately, Gulliver's adventures will break his spirit. Finally, back in England, he spends his dotage glumly reminiscing of the strange, far-off lands he encountered in his youth. The inhabitants of Nuyts Land, he thinks, could teach Europeans a thing or two about respect and the proper way to live honourably.

# CHAPTER 4
## A Time in Versailles

The photographs get it wrong. In every one of Eugène Atget's studies of Versailles from the 1900s, the Palace grounds are gloomy, silent and deserted, as though the inhabitants suddenly and inexplicably hurried away one night, as though the over-wrought buildings, the carefully cultivated gardens, the pathways leading through wooded groves to small, precisely formed, classical monuments never needed people in the first place. Versailles, Atget is saying, has always been here, ignorant of time.

Back in the 1900s, however, people *wrote* that in high summer Versailles was crowded with tourists from across Europe and America. They travelled to Paris with its restaurants and museums, but Versailles was the highlight, and they walked between rooms in the palace, speaking in reverent whispers, a hum like swarms of butterflies. Some had come to compare this monument against their own ruined histories. They stood in front of paintings with notebooks open, nervously scribbling in pencil. Others weren't so shy about their anxieties. They wanted to believe that a small, glistening scrap of the palace's aura rubbed off on their souls. To pass slowly from painting to painting, conscientiously reading the meaning in each, was to become a better person, for an afternoon anyway. It was also a good place to preen, to stand in front of a sculpture and tell anyone within a two-metre radius some anecdote perhaps associated with its creator. And it was a place to be overcome, to suddenly feel the compulsion to sit on the marble benches and madly fan the face, as though the early August heat was the cause of this distress.

Strange then that in high summer the crowded Palace was also listless. The humidity, the gnats swarming above the rose beds, the damp clinging to every scrap of fabric that touched the skin, and all the art in all the rooms, all the light glittering off gilt frames through all the prisms of crystal; it all beat down any levity. This was not a place for humour, beyond the usual dry quips about Louis XIV's high-heels or his bouffant. Even these effortless wisecracks were murmured rather than spoken, at levels reserved for churches or libraries.

The people came to experience Ancien Régime Paris as if the poverty, the filth, the smallpox, the syphilis and typhoid, the dead in the streets, the palpable anger of ordinary citizens never existed. In this recreation of Versailles everyone was a powdered minor noble or a louche intellectual, travelling about in sculptured carriages, ruminating on the philosophy of gardening or attending balls in the Hall of Mirrors. This history allowed no logic to the Revolution; that was more like a cancer, which erupted then destroyed without offering any meaning.

The myth sustained Versailles. The rigorous symmetry of the architecture and the exuberance of the art smothered any possibility of a debate about taste or even talent. The world beyond the palace's walls belonged somewhere else; so far away that just to wonder about it felt heretical.

Which is why, on the afternoon of August 10, 1901, Charlotte Moberly and Eleanor Jourdain wanted to escape, to take in the sticky humidity of the gardens as a release from all that relentless opulence.

They walked away from the Palace, towards the Petit Trianon, Marie Antoinette's small palace situated in the gardens a short distance to the east of the Grand Trianon.

Charlotte Moberly described it this way:

We walked briskly forward, talking as before, but from the moment we left the lane an extraordinary depression had come over me, which, in spite of every effort to shake off, steadily deepened. There seemed to be absolutely no reason for it; I was not at all tired, and was becoming more interested in my surroundings. I was anxious that my companion should not discover the sudden gloom upon my spirits, which became quite overpowering on reaching the point where the path ended, being crossed by another, right and left.

In front of us was a wood, within which, and overshadowed by trees, was a light garden kiosk, circular, and like a small bandstand, by which a man was sitting.

Eleanor Jourdain recalled things differently:

I saw a gate leading to a path cut deep below the level of the ground above, and as the way was open and had the look of an entrance that was used, I said, 'Shall we try this path? It must lead to the house,' and we followed it. To our right we saw some farm-buildings looking empty and deserted; implements (among others a plough) were lying about; we looked in, but saw no one.

Charlotte Moberly: *There were three paths in front of us, and as we saw two men a little ahead on the centre one, we followed it, and asked them the way. Afterwards we spoke of them as gardeners, because we remembered a wheelbarrow of some kind close by and the look of a pointed spade, but they were really very dignified officials, dressed in long greyish green coats with small three-cornered hats. They directed us straight on.*

Eleanor Jourdain: *There were two men there in official dress (greenish in colour), with something in their hands; it might have been a staff. A wheelbarrow and some other gardening tools were near them. They told us, in answer to my enquiry, to go straight on. I remember repeating my question, because they answered in a seemingly casual and mechanical way, but only got the same answer in the same manner.*

The women continued on their way, each privately suspecting a strangeness in the atmosphere yet unaware the other shared it. Eleanor Jourdain later wrote that she began to feel like she was walking in her sleep.

\*

Their portraits aren't quite right either. Charlotte Moberly was fifty-five in 1901. The best-known depiction of her is an 1899 oil painting by William Llewellyn, who was at the beginning of a prosperous, otherwise unremarkable career as a society portraitist. Moberly was the principal at St Hugh's, the women's college at Oxford founded by Elizabeth Wordsworth in 1886. There is something intimidating and haughty in her expression. This was a painting intended to be hung in a hall, where generations of students were expected to draw from its spirit and gravitas.[8]

She was comfortable with power. Her father was George Moberly, Bishop of Salisbury, a seat that placed him close to the inner sanctum of the Anglican church. It was a tight, even incestuous world; when he died in 1885, he was succeeded by John Wordsworth, Elizabeth's brother. Of his seven sons, four became clerics, and among his eight daughters one married a cleric while Charlotte's position as Principal at St Hugh's required judicious politicking with the church authorities.

It doesn't help that photographs of Anglican ministers from the late Victorian era show stout, grey-haired men like George Moberly, or gaunt, balding ones like John Wordsworth: grim-faced and austere whatever the shape. The feeling from both is of a stultifying, joyless world, but years later the writer and former student of Charlotte Moberly, Edith Olivier, described her teacher's childhood as "fun and games and habitual merriment, animation and playfulness" and "full of interest in everything, tender kindness, cheerfulness, and keen, bright wit."

It could be assumed from this (and considering the course his daughter's life took) that George Moberly was a progressive, but it's more accurate to think of him as a pragmatist, who understood the inevitability of change, so whatever he thought of higher education for women (not much according to some sources), he also knew that the arguments opposed to it were bound to fall. In any case, Charlotte Moberly's mother, Mary

---

[8] St Hugh's was hardly a hotbed of radical feminism. Elizabeth Wordsworth once claimed the ideal woman could not be a bore because she never overworked her brain.

Anne Crokat, was the driving force in the rearing of the daughters. Raised in Italy and described (by Edith Olivier again) as 'the Beauty of Naples', she home-schooled her daughters in languages, music and philosophy. The job prospects might be limited but the girls would emerge fully formed as cultured beings. When Charlotte wrote a hagiography of her father, *Dulce Domum*, it was primarily a love letter to her mother, the source of the fun, the games and interest in everything in the Moberly household.

In 1901 Eleanor Jourdain was thirty-seven but the most common portrait of her is a standard studio photograph taken around 1911, when she was much closer in age to the Charlotte Moberly in Llewellyn's painting. Her intent, penetrating expression burns through her drab surroundings. She came from the same Anglican world as Charlotte Moberly, but a couple of rungs lower socially, and if Charlotte had been raised to think of education as morally uplifting, Eleanor clung to it as a way out of financial struggle and ordinariness. By the time of the photograph, she had earned one degree in history at Lady Margaret Hall at Oxford and her doctorate at the University of Paris in 1904, writing her theses on the use of symbolism in Dante's *Inferno*. That made her preposterously over-qualified for a world that only wanted to offer her occasional work as a governess or French tutor. St Hugh's presented one of the scarce alternatives.

The trip to Versailles is sometimes described as an elaborate job interview, with Charlotte appraising Eleanor to take on the upcoming position as vice-principal, but the vacancy wasn't coming up for fifteen years and even if it was, they could have counted the competition on one hand with fingers to spare. How many other women in Britain had doctorates in Renaissance literature, which they had written in French, sitting alongside their other published works on metaphysics and French drama? And how many other sympathetic ears would she find?

And if the Anglican hierarchy was all about networks, St Hugh's was a smaller world but more intense for that. Charlotte Moberly had been one of the first five students to enrol in the College, alongside Eleanor's sister, Annie. All the women that play a part in the account that follows were either students or teachers at St Hugh's, or had a close relationship to someone from there.

Between the two, Eleanor Jourdain is the more interesting. Partly it is timing; she is at the beginning of her career while Charlotte Moberly is already conscious retirement looms, which must be read into the two portraits. But really, the difference is more subtle and mysterious. One is yet to have the experience at Versailles, the other has been radically transformed by it.

\*

The place was so shut in that we could not see beyond it. Everything suddenly looked unnatural, therefore unpleasant; even the trees behind the building seemed to have become flat and lifeless, like a wood worked in tapestry. There were no effects of light and shade, and no wind stirred the trees. It was all intensely still.

Charlotte Moberly's creeping unease was still subliminal, a feeling that the world was wrong but not yet untethered.

That was about to ratchet up as they approached a small kiosk.

The man sitting close to the kiosk (who had on a cloak and a large shady hat) turned his head and looked at us. That was the culmination of my peculiar sensations, and I felt a moment of genuine alarm. The man's face was most repulsive - its expression odious. His complexion was very dark and rough.

Eleanor Jourdain's impressions were close enough to support Charlotte Moberly's, down to the revulsion she felt as the man looked up at them.

At that moment the eerie feeling which had begun in the garden culminated in a definite impression of something uncanny and fear-inspiring. The man slowly turned his face, which was marked by smallpox: his complexion was very dark. The expression was very evil and yet unseeing, and though I did not feel that he was looking particularly at us, I felt a repugnance to going past him.

Nothing will induce me to go to the left, Charlotte Moberly thought, and: It was a great relief at that moment to hear someone running up to us in breathless haste. Connecting the sound with the gardeners, I turned and ascertained that there was no one on the paths, either to the side or behind, but at almost the same moment I suddenly perceived another man quite close to us, behind and rather to the left hand, who had, apparently, just come either over or through the rock (or whatever it was) that shut out the view at the junction of the paths. The suddenness of his appearance was something of a shock.

Eleanor Jourdain also experienced that sense of aural dislocation but, though she also saw the man, went one better and communicated with him.

He shouted, 'Mesdames, mesdames,' and when I turned he said in an accent that seemed to me unusual that our way lay in another direction. 'Il ne faut (pronounced fout) 'pas passer par là.' He then made a gesture, adding, 'par ici...cherchez la maison.' Though we were surprised to be addressed, we were glad of the direction, and I thanked him. The man ran off with a curious smile on his face: the running ceased as abruptly as it had begun, not far from where we stood. I remember that the man was young-looking, with a florid complexion and rather long dark hair. I do not remember the dress, except that the material was dark and heavy, and that the man wore buckled shoes.

This marked the point where both women recognized that the world around them had somehow freed itself from tangible reality, but it is also the point where the reader feels suspicions take hold, the way a magistrate might hearing two witnesses who have obviously rehearsed their lines.

Charlotte Moberly: *Silently we passed over the small rustic bridge which crossed a tiny ravine. So close to us when on the bridge that we could have touched it with our right hands, a thread-like cascade fell from a height down a green pretty bank, where ferns grew between stones. Where the little trickle of water went to I did not see, but it gave me the impression that we were near other water, though I saw none.*

Eleanor Jourdain: *We walked on, crossing a small bridge that went across a green bank, high on our right hand and shelving down below as to a very small overshadowed pool of water glimmering some way off. A tiny stream descended from above us, so small as to seem to lose itself before reaching the little pool. We then followed a narrow path till almost immediately we came upon the English garden in front of the Petit Trianon. The place was deserted; but as we approached the terrace I remember drawing my skirt away with a feeling as though someone were near and I had to make room.*

"Do you think," Charlotte Moberly asked Eleanor Jourdain a week later, "Versailles is haunted?"

\*

Every problem with this incident has to do with time. For starters, there's the week delay between the visit to the Palace and Charlotte Moberly's question, suggesting she'd been anticipating what Eleanor Jourdain's answer would be, then the months that passed before they compared notes, then the years, an entire decade, before they published their account. That was enough time to research, to contemplate, to reconsider small details and suddenly recall others, slightly different to how they may have first been remembered. More than enough time really to take a dizzy spell and redraft it into a brief but vivid journey into the past.

And there was that, too. It took no great imagination in the 1910s to construct a haunting: every writer from the lowest hack to the brightest star was trying their hand at ghost stories, but the scenario the women proposed was not the standard case of wandering through old buildings and encountering the manifestation of someone who had died. Rather, it was as though there was a tear in the fabric of time that allowed them to enter the gardens of Versailles at some point just before August 1792 and walk among people going about their daily business. Effectively the two women were claiming they were the ghosts.

On paper, they were impeccable witnesses: educated, cultivated, with reputations too valuable to squander on a tall story; all good reasons to publish *An Adventure* in 1911 under the pseudonyms Elizabeth Morison and Frances Lamont.

That took them ten years because they were also academics, who never wrote a sentence without worrying over its weaknesses. And they were busy, especially Eleanor Jourdain. In the years between the incident and the publication of their account, she earned her doctorate, took up her position at St Hugh's, mobilized suffragettes for rallies, published papers on biblical exegesis, symbolism in *The Inferno* and pedagogy in France, and two of her lectures had been collected in *On the Theory of the Infinite in Modern Thought*.

There are a few adjectives that come to mind reading the lectures. Unnecessary is one: her arguments that there was a divide between metaphysics and mathematics were dubious then, irrelevant now that no-one in the game thinks of either discipline as distinct. Intimidating is another. She assumes the reader needs no introduction to Plato, Kant, Descartes, Thomas Aquinas, Hegel, Pascal, Saint Augustine and Leibniz, which says something about the standards she expected from her students.

Leaving aside the French neo-critical School (Renouvier) and the English School (Spencer) the first of whom deny the Infinite, thus acting in opposition to mathematical reasoning, while the second perpetuate Kant's error of considering the Infinite, though thinkable, as unknowable (Dr. Caird has pointed out that this position is illogical) we arrive at a moment in history which is more fruitful in result on the mathematical side, and will, no doubt, have an effect on metaphysics.

The Infinite capitalized usually refers to a supreme being, an agent of human desires, but Eleanor Jourdain was thinking along even more abstract lines. Her Infinite was the nexus between time and space. The task facing philosophers and mathematicians was to locate that and give it coherence. Do so and the world and its human occupants made sense.

Or it might anyway to someone who believed that she'd been given a glimpse of that nexus.

*Does our world contain facts of other dimensions?* She asked that having already given her answer a few lines earlier. *If there did not exist a fourth dimension, we could not be aware of a third as such.*

Orthodox thinkers insisted that time followed the Newtonian model. It was an unwavering arrow that could be measured travelling between two points, which explained why the sun rose and set at predictable times, why people grew old (and died), why it was always too late to go back and put right the mistakes you made. But when time was fixed it left questions that couldn't be answered. If time could be measured moving through space, what was space made up of? If the Newtonian model was right, it had to be uniform, but Newton himself had proposed gravity, which experts understood was just one force that altered uniformity.

She gave her second lecture in 1908, knowing that if the problem hadn't been solved it was in capable hands. In the 1860s, James Clerk Maxwell had proposed that light travelled in waves, and since the speed of light established one boundary of time that left Newtonian time already looking redundant. The Americans Charles Hinton and Cassius Keyser had separately tackled the problem of multi-dimensionality in time (Hinton back in the 1880s). In France, Henri Poincaré had taken a rigorously mathematical approach and Henri Bergson had thought of time in terms of perception. The Dutch physicists Lorentz and Zeeman won the Nobel Prize in 1902 for discovering the Zeeman effect on the frequency of light, and a year later Bertrand Russell had published *The Principles of Mathematics* (but not yet *Principia Mathematica*). By 1905, when Einstein published two papers, *On the Electrodynamics of Moving Bodies* and *Does the Inertia of a Body Depend Upon Its Energy Content?* time looked vague and uncertain, and wide open to interpretation. Eleanor Jourdain made no mention of either paper in her lectures, but then Einstein's former teacher Hermann Minkowski had been one of only a handful who understood the ramifications of both on theories of spacetime; for most people they were mere words on paper.

Eleanor Jourdain may not have been able to make sense of Einstein, but she was aware that the problem of time was not as ineffable as ordinary people might believe, even when the logic that philosophers and mathematicians confronted it with appeared impenetrable. Time followed laws we could not understand. It could be elastic, and it could behave erratically.

She knew that because she had been privileged with a personal revelation.

Every idea Eleanor Jourdain articulated in *On the Theory of the Infinite in Modern Thought* could be traced back to that afternoon at Versailles. Not that her audience would have known this. She delivered her lecture a good two years before she and Charlotte Moberly published *An Adventure*, and though she had often discussed what happened at Versailles with friends and her students, she'd been circumspect, in the same way she was in the lectures. Mathematicians understood the mechanical intricacies of time, and philosophers could see how their rules misbehaved. What if, she mused, the two came together: how truly strange and wonderful time might turn out to be. What, she was really asking, had happened to me that day?

So far the two women are witnesses, but not suspects. Maybe there's a layer to the events they ignored, or overlooked, but no one has to think they are liars to doubt their stories. Not yet, anyway.

They walk alongside a neglected and overgrown meadow. The clouds are white but there's a dampness in the air that fills Charlotte Moberly with despondency, like the late Autumn showers around Oxford. As they turn a bend a small two-storey house comes into view. It's an old house; the ornate wooden shutters on the top floor are closed. The lawns have been let wild. They follow a path around a corner and:

> a lady was sitting, holding out a paper as though to look at it at arm's length. I supposed her to be sketching, and to have brought her own camp-stool. It seemed as though she must be making a study of trees...there seemed to be

nothing else to sketch. She saw us, and when we passed close by on her left hand, she turned and looked full at us. It was not a young face, and (though rather pretty) it did not attract me.

Charlotte Moberly describes the woman's outfit in detail: bodice, skirts, broad brimmed sun hat. She thinks at that moment the woman must be a tourist. They walk up the steps to the terrace when she looks down she sees the woman from a different view. Again, she describes her outfit; it's straight out of the 1780s. Charlotte Moberly has that inkling of disquiet she felt earlier on. So:

*It was rather a relief to me that Miss Lamont did not propose to ask her whether we could enter the house from that side.*

That would have been difficult. Eleanor Jourdain didn't see anyone to ask.

Charlotte Moberly's subsequent research would leave her in no doubt who the woman was, and you have to agree; what would be the point in two Edwardian scholars going back in time to Versailles 1792 if it wasn't to see Marie Antoinette? But what gives the encounter the sniff of authenticity is its banality. There's no sense of impending disaster about the woman, none of the terror of hunted prey, only a woman drawing, on a day like any other. The sketching woman isn't the smoking gun, she's the witness who disappeared, the one who holds all the answers, if only she could be found again.

The place was deserted; but as we approached the terrace I remember drawing my skirt away with a feeling as though someone were near and I had to make room, and then wondering why I did it. While we were on the terrace a boy came out of the door of a second building which opened on it, and I still have the sound in my ears of his slamming it behind him. He directed us to go round to the other entrance, and, seeing us hesitate, with the peculiar smile of suppressed mockery offered to show us the way.

The slamming of the door behind him was a sign for the women to return to reality, the way a hypnotist might click his fingers. After watching a wedding party in progress, they caught a carriage away from the Palace to the Hôtel des Réservoirs, where they had tea, neither inclined to say much.

*

Later, when the real identities of Elizabeth Morison and Frances Lamont had been exposed and their account picked over by eager theorizers, it would become an article of faith that *An Adventure* caused a sensation when it first came out in 1911, but what happened at the time was much more prosaic.

"A remarkable psychological experience", the *Civil and Military Gazette* in Lahore reported in February 1911, which, given the English taste for anything odd or exotic coming out of the subcontinent, sounded somewhat patronising in its assumption the event had happened inside the women's heads.

*The Yorkshire Post and Leeds Intelligencer* was dismissive the way it might be with a dodgy solution to a murder mystery: "There is a pretty psychological problem in 'The Adventure' (sic) that no amount of discussion can solve."

*The Queen*, AKA *The Ladies Newspaper and Court Chronicle*, thought it would at least appeal to followers of popular occultists: "WE believe that any readers of this little book who are familiar with the writings of Mrs Verrall or of Miss Alice Johnson which have been published by the Society for Psychical Research, will at once be struck by the resemblance in style – not so much literary style, but (if we may invent an expression) in style of mind."

Unflappability was a fashionable Edwardian trait, but no one was willing to come off the fence and endorse the book. They could have without risking too much shame. The Victorian passion for contact with the other side had not abated. People still attended seances in suburban houses and watched mediums vomit up gauze or lined up outside fairground tents to hear messages from the recently departed. The Society for Psychical Research had been led by well-known philosophers like William James and Henry Sidgwick, who gave credibility to the idea that the world beyond could be approached with the same scientific rigour as this earthly one, and some of its most famous cases had ended with an unresolved finding (which meant, for too many readers, solved on the side of the ghosts).

But perhaps the critics found the book a tad dull. There was some stiff competition from the twilight world between this and the other side, and despite the SPR's efforts to be professional and objective, it remained the best source for gripping accounts of psychic phenomena. In the tangled maze of a Naples slum, Eusapia Palladino sat in a darkened room, with colourful sparks flashing sporadically behind her and odd sounds coming out from the shadows, while she wrote messages with her finger on client's arms. The messages materialized as though written in pencil. The report by Frederic Myers and Oliver Lodge had a modern creepiness: a woman who had never known her parents, or any kind of love, or education for that, yet possessed a humble saint's superpower, and the imprimatur of the world's leading researchers into the paranormal. Meanwhile Catherine Muller, alias Hélène Smith, entered a trance state and described a long pedigree of bodies she had inhabited, including Marie Antoinette's. She also spoke Martian. Slightly before the time of the Society for Psychical Research, David Dunglas Hume used to levitate pianos and have them float about rooms while music played. He himself used to grow a couple of feet in length during seances. If the readers didn't believe any of that, part of them ached for some part to be true.

Eleanor Sidgwick, wife of Henry Sidgwick, President of the Society for Psychical Research, wrote one of the harshest reviews of *An Adventure*, claiming without much need to go into detail that it simply didn't happen. Her review stung: she was not just another principal of a women's college, Newnham at Cambridge, but she had a background in electrophysics so she was a first among equals though she was never going to abide any proposals that ignored scientific method.

She didn't have to know the identities of the authors of *An Adventure* to tell they were women with respectable positions. Like good novelists, they spoke with a measured pace and the general attitude among the reviewers was that it ranked alongside boilerplate ghost stories: interesting for devotees but hardly likely to set the rest of the world on fire.

There had to be some demand because it was reprinted five times then brought out in a new edition in 1913, with additions, and always with a disclaimer from the publisher: "The ladies whose Adventure is described in these pages have for various reasons preferred not to disclose their real names, but the signatures appended to the Preface are the only fictitious words in the book."

That was standard protection for authors and publishers when aliases were used, but it was a common practice with fictional ghost stories too, where the pseudonym subtly implied some factual aspect real people wanted hidden. Alternatively, names could be obscured like so: "I was enjoying brandy and cigars at the club with Lord D—when he casually mentioned he'd had an encounter with a ghost". An alias let it be known that while this was fiction, there might be a grain of truth to it, as if using a real name was going to get threatening letters from the lawyers. The obscured name spoke the truth without committing to it. The women used the same device further on in the book: *On Monday, July 4th, 1904, Miss Lamont and I went to the Trianon, this being my second visit. We were accompanied by Mademoiselle ——, who had not heard our story.*

But the disclaimer carried the impression it was one more invented detail among the pages to come.

There were other problems. Towards the end the authors wrote: *Both of us have inherited a horror of all forms of occultism. We lose no opportunity of preaching against them as unwholesome and misleading.*

Of course, they needed to say that, but it contradicted the whole preceding paragraph.

One of us has to own to having powers of second sight, etc., deliberately undeveloped, and there are psychical gifts in her family. She comes of a Huguenot stock. The other is one of a large and cheerful party, being the seventh daughter and of a seventh son; her mother and grandmother were entirely Scotch, and both possessed powers of premonition accompanied by vision.

Not only leading the reader into the realm of folklore, but doing it with non-sequiturs as well.

That wasn't all.

We were entirely ignorant of the history and traditions of the place, and continued our conversation about other things after every interruption. We did not even know that we were in the grounds of the Petit Trianon until we saw the house.

Which wasn't true. Charlotte Moberly wrote (under her pseudonym): *My knowledge of French history was limited to the very little I had learnt in the schoolroom, historical novels, and the first volume of Justin McCarthy's French Revolution. Over thirty years before my brother had written a prize poem on Marie Antoinette, for whom at the time I had felt much enthusiasm.*

So actually she knew a bit, or rather, enough. And:

I suggested our going to the Petit Trianon. My sole knowledge of it was from a magazine article read as a girl, from which I received a general impression that it was a farmhouse where the Queen had amused herself.

Then there was Chapter IV, *A Reverie*, that began as an academic enquiry into the French Revolution but morphed into a literary meditation on the last months of Marie Antoinette's life.

Was the penury of the country and the starving condition of the poor at the bottom of this earthquake? But why visit them upon the Court? People must know that she and the King were most kindly and anxious and troubled for all. They had reduced every possible expense in their household. Had she not nine years ago refused the diamond necklace on account of its expense?

That paragraph sounded like two dowdy spinsters with a taste for the paranormal concocting one more airless tale about the ghost of their favourite historical character. The wonder is that so many newspapers bothered to review it.

The 1913 edition was an improvement on the first. Every dubious statement remained but sections were moved about, and the addition of maps and an appendix gave it weight, leaving the reader in no doubt anymore that this was an account of a supposedly actual event.

On the train back to Paris, Charlotte Moberly looked out the window towards the Palace.

> …the setting sun at last burst out from under the clouds, bathing the distant Versailles woods in glowing light, – Valerien standing out in front a mass of deep purple. Again and again the thought returned, – Was Marie Antoinette really much at Trianon, and did she see it for the last time long before the fatal drive to Paris accompanied by the mob?

*

Five months later, on January 10, 1902, Eleanor Jourdain returned to Versailles, to reconnoitre with the ghosts again, which she had to, because if she didn't all the theories distilling in her head would have come to nothing.

Tourists avoided Versailles in the winter; most would have merely been exchanging one cold, wet town for another, and January was only the best time to walk through the gardens if you wanted to be alone, just your thoughts and ideas for company. The morning's rain dripped sporadically from the branches where it had been trapped, the sodden brown leaves matting the paths so even her sensible walking shoes were damp. The cold was insidious the way it penetrated her cloak, but not so unforgiving to drive off the squirrels and other small mammals rummaging through the humus. She ignored them. There was a bigger problem than the weather. When she hurried to the Temple de l'Amour, near the kiosk where the repulsive man with smallpox pits had looked up at them, a different building, the one on the modern tourist maps, stood in its place. This was disconcerting, suddenly the world was as it should be, but all was not lost.

> …On crossing a bridge to go to the Hameau, the old feeling returned in full force; it was as if I had crossed a line and was suddenly in a circle of influence. To the left I saw a tract of park-like ground, the trees bare and very scanty.

Atget knew why winter was the best time to visit the gardens. It brought the ghosts out. For all its opulence, Versailles was a sombre and gloomy place. Call that the weight of history; what happened here in the 1790s shook up countries where people didn't speak French, let alone understand the politics. Colour and light didn't do justice to that, but grim skies, bare, skeletal trees and the absence of people could, especially the absence of people. Excluding them gave viewers the liberty to imagine their own presences, and whether these were courtly types from the eighteenth century or something more contemporary, it didn't matter. With a really effective haunting the point wasn't to see people but to be aware of them.

> I noticed a cart being filled with sticks by two labourers, and thought I could go to them for directions if I lost my way. The men wore tunics and capes with pointed hoods of bright colours, a sort of terra-cotta red and deep blue.

She is not quite saying the two are phantoms, only there is something anachronistic about their dress, and even that is a matter of interpretation. Being a scholar, Eleanor Jourdain might never have tried her hand at fiction but she knew the rules, how to sprinkle the beginning of a narrative with hints and vague promises, and how to deliver, not with a shock but with creeping disconcertion.

> I was puzzling my way among the maze of paths in the wood when I heard a rustling behind me which made me wonder why people in silk dresses came out on such a wet day; and I said to myself, "just like French people." I turned sharply round to see who they were, but saw no one.

Back in August she and Charlotte Moberly had experienced the sensation of hearing invisible footfalls and whispered voices so, though for a moment it was as if the voices surrounded her, she didn't feel the slightest fear.

> I heard some women's voices talking French, and caught the words "Monsieur et Madame" said close to my ear.

The crowd got scarce and drifted away, and then faint music as of a band, not far off, was audible. It was playing very light music with a good deal of repetition in it. Both voices and music were diminished in tone, as in a phonograph, unnaturally. The pitch of the band was lower than usual. The sounds were intermittent, and once more I felt the swish of a dress close by me.

If one encounter with the metaphysical past sounded enthralling, repeating it could only be preposterous, but ghosts, she knew, never carried messages. They drifted, bemused and as baffled by the familiar as ordinary mortals.

She left Versailles, her conviction some mysterious energy was at work confirmed, though it would have taken something really dramatic to persuade her otherwise.

Later that week, Parisian friends told her of a legend that Marie Antoinette could sometimes be seen working the butter churn in the small annexe by her chateau where milk had been turned into butter, cream and cheese. Not proof perhaps, but pointing in that direction.

And she kept coming back: once with Charlotte Moberly in 1904, and at other times with friends or alone. Seventy years later the art historian Joan Evans described a trip to Versailles with her mother, the classicist Maria Lathbury and Eleanor Jourdain in 1910, a year before the book came out. They were there to take photographs of the gardens for research, Evans claiming that by then (she was twelve or thirteen) she was already sick of hearing about the ghosts at Versailles.

Evans in her way is one more ghost in this story, haunting its edges as a passive observer, waiting for her moment to step up and lay it to rest with lethal intent.

Later, of course, people, their colleagues and students, the ones who had shared their ideas and called on them for help when it was needed, would declare both women were outside the mainstream. Eleanor Jourdain especially had weird ideas and an intensity about her that was off-putting, but in January 1915 the world's longest job interview ended when Charlotte Moberly retired as Principal of Saint Hugh's and Eleanor Jourdain was appointed as her successor. That same month Reverend Henry Ady died. Among the mourners at the service in Ockham, Surrey, were Mary, Countess of Lovelace, the sculptor Mary Frances Tytler, Henry Scott-Holland, Regius Professor of Divinity at Oxford, a viscount, a general and various other reverends, so a respectable mix of upper middle class English society, minor nobility, intellectuals, bohemians and arch-conservatives. St Hugh's sent a wreath to the service, not so much out of respect for the dead but for one of the College's best and brightest tutors, his daughter Cecilia Mary.

Like Charlotte Moberly, she didn't choose her career so much as follow a well-signed path. Though her mother was technically untrained as an art historian, she had understood that a veneer of knowledge was a mark of good breeding and written a small library's worth of books, articles and pamphlets on Renaissance painters. Highbrow scholars (like her daughter) didn't put much value in Julia Cartwright Ady's work but the people who wanted a few facts with a dash of measured opinion to show off their culture lapped her up.

By 1915 Cecilia was the woman her mother might have wanted to be. At 34, she had already published a serious history of Renaissance Milan and a biography of the Renaissance humanist Pope Pius II and she belonged to a small, emerging group of historians who argued culture rather than individuals was the driving force in history. While her mother read a few books and looked at a lot of paintings, Cecilia Ady went to the archives, found documents and analysed them. Her intellectual energy was immense and it's no surprise she became one of Eleanor Jourdain's closest friends, so close the fallout was as inevitable as it was brutal.

The Edwardian world of women's colleges wasn't cloistered (even if a fair number of the residents longed for a world without men) but it was insular, like a network that kept feeding back on itself. Over at St Hilda's the Principal was Winifred Moberly. At Holloway College at the University of London, future novelist Ivy Compton-Burnett (descendent of a Bishop of Salisbury) was studying classics when she met Margaret Jourdain, then at Eleanor's old college, Lady Margaret Hall. They would soon move in together to live as 'companions', one of those expressions people could interpret how they wanted though it was usually reserved for fusty eccentrics who didn't care what others thought. Margaret Jourdain knew Joan Evans (Half-sister of Arthur Evans, who had discovered Knossos on Crete a few years earlier) and pushed her to pursue an education, which she did, finding work as a librarian at St Hugh's.

In 1920 the commercial artist Wilton Williams drew two illustrations to accompany an article about the women's colleges at Oxford. In the first, they play hockey (outdoor sports, good). The second has them indoors, not in class, or studying but attending demure tea parties (also good). God knows what they are supposed to be talking about, it looks like nothing at all. If he had actually set foot in St Hugh's, the picture he would have drawn would have been rancorous, combative and nurturing in equal measure.

Joan Evans's assessment of Eleanor Jourdain at St Hugh's puts it in perspective. *A curious and baffling personality, as far as I can judge a psychological egoist, absorbed in her own mental and emotional processes.* Today that sounds like textbook narcissism, but it was another way for Evans to imply the new principal was the engineer of her own demise. By 'curious and baffling' and 'absorbed in her own mental and emotional processes', Evans was alluding to the intense metaphysical quest that Eleanor Jourdain had embarked upon nearly two decades earlier, the same that others would pin as fundamental to her fallout with Cecilia Ady.

Archives are receptacles of disinterested evidence, documents that have the power to destroy lives but cannot intrinsically possess malicious intent. Only the people who use them make use of that, but for professional historians, malice against the past is pointless when the subject and its actors have been dead for centuries. Cecilia Ady understood that. The proper way to approach the history of the Renaissance was practical; she could speculate on actors' motives, but there had to be evidence to support her theories. This approach depended upon objective detachment. Her mother was the opposite – the figures who passed through her books were heroes driven by powerful, romantic impulses. So was Eleanor Jourdain: her passion was ideas, which didn't need evidence to anchor them to reality. At some point the historian wearied of metaphysics' frivolity, or she resented the way it achieved respect without requiring the physical proof she was obliged to produce, or she simply no longer believed Eleanor Jourdain's stories.

Anybody who has been to university has witnessed Sayre's law at work: the fights are so nasty because the stakes are so low. Sometimes they simmer along for years, to the degree bystanders assume the participants must enjoy quietly crucifying each other, but other times they erupt so brutally that one of the cardinal rules of academic life gets broken. The press get wind and begin circling.

Every four years at St Hugh's the tutors' commission came to an end and they reapplied for the position. This was well before academic tenure became a concept, but it was a formality that the reapplication would be accepted. In December 1923 Cecelia Ady's term expired, and Eleanor Jourdain did not reappoint her. Their colleagues were already aware that there was trouble between the two but that sent shockwaves through the college.

Cecilia Ady was incredibly popular with students and staff. For years, history had a reputation for being run by dusty old men welded to some rusted out methodologies. Students still had to read Thomas Carlyle but that didn't mean they had to talk like him. Cecilia Ady was modern and so were her ideas. If Eleanor Jourdain wanted to pick a fight or prove a point, she couldn't have chosen a worse target. The response of the five female tutors, then several male members of the college council, was to immediately resign. That was when the press moved in.

By our standards the reporting was polite, but headlines like "Trouble at Girls' College" or "Tutorial Revolt at Oxford" were bad enough. A formal inquiry was called. Its importance to Oxford could be measured by the man who led it, the Chancellor of Oxford, George, 1$^{st}$ Marquess of Curzon, previously Secretary of State, Lord President of the Council and Viceroy of India, not so adept at cleaning messes perhaps but a fixed idea of what needed to be done. The result was quick and efficient as a guillotine. Cynthia Ady was reinstated. Eleanor Jourdain resigned.

Within weeks she fell dead from a heart attack.

The obituaries praised her academic and intellectual achievements, *philosopher, artist, musician, an able administrator with good business abilities, a clear headed writer and scholar,* a couple made vague reference to recent troubles at St Hugh's. Only the *Daily Mirror* was willing to remind readers why they otherwise might have heard of her.

> In none of the obituary notices of Miss Jourdain, principal of St. Hugh's College, Oxford, was it mentioned that she, with Miss Moberly, her predecessor, had an experience remarkable enough to be published by Macmillan's under the title " An Adventure."

*

In 1884 a frail and pallid nine-year-old boy called out from his bed to his nurse. He had a question. This was in Belgravia, a part of London where most children were cared for by nannies and the weaker ones had a nurse, and it was an age when the standard treatment for any childhood illness or injury was to stay in bed on the off chance it would pass. Bedrooms were a petri dish for precocious children drawn to obscure musings and John William Dunne was torn between the muffled sounds of life outside the curtained windows and the vivid interiors of his own mind.

The question he wanted his nurse to answer was how to define time: past, present *and* future, or should the conjunction be '*or*'? We don't know her name but it's a fair guess she couldn't tell him; if she was at all typical of domestic help, she found ailing child philosophers in their dimly lit bedrooms acutely annoying.

But he didn't forget the question. He came from a military family and after a disappointing service record, pensioned off with more infirmities, he turned to aircraft design. This was before the Wright Brothers launched their flyer at Kill Devil Hills in 1903: hundreds were out there designing aircraft, a few well ahead of the brothers when it came to understanding principles of aeronautics. Dunne was among that number. The brothers weren't yet airborne and he could already see the advantages of swept wing design in increasing stability, so much that he could design a plane without tail wings. It looked like two stacked boomerangs, and in 1913 it flew across the English Channel. Had he treated his question about time as nothing more than a child's fancy, he would be remembered today as a brilliant engineer whose influential research extended beyond the Jumbo and the Concorde to the Stealth Bomber. He didn't, so instead, from the 1920s into the 1930s, he was a world-famous mystic/philosopher, who used mathematical logic in a way that intimidated critics of his most esoteric ideas. Instead of a line connecting him to the Wright brothers, it would be drawn back to Eleanor Jourdain.

For years Dunne had been bothered by dreams that appeared to foretell the future; well before designing his first aircraft he had a dream he was sitting in a flying machine. He was staying at a hotel in Sussex in 1898 when he dreamed he was arguing with a waiter about the time. Specifically, his watch had stopped at half past four but while he insisted it had stopped in the afternoon the waiter was adamant it had stopped early morning. Dunne woke up and looked at his watch. It had stopped, at four thirty: morning or afternoon it didn't matter.

In January 1901, Dunne was in Alassio, between Nice and Genoa on the Ligurian coast when he had another dream. He was on the Nile, not far from Khartoum, when three bedraggled and badly sunburnt British soldiers emerged from the desert. They reminded him of soldiers in his company in South Africa where he had served briefly before illness again took him out. He was curious what they were doing in the Sudan and they explained they had just walked from the Cape: "Awful time," one said. "Nearly died from yellow fever".

At breakfast that morning Dunne opened the latest edition of the *Daily Telegraph* (at least a week old by this time), to read that the expedition from Cape Town had just arrived in Khartoum, minus one soldier who had died from yellow fever.

First published in 1927, *An Experiment with Time* was a book the world asked for in strange and uncertain times but it still caught publishers unprepared. The core of Dunne's theory (time was fluid and the evidence for that could be found in dreams) was a concoction of essences of the two most trailblazing and subversive thinkers of the age, Freud (the unconscious) and Einstein (time), in a way that skipped the complexity and put infinite possibility within reach. You didn't have to read either (let alone understand them) to take these principles, apply them to *An Experiment with Time* and see how, metaphysically speaking, a few gentle prods could get reality behaving in odd and unpredictable ways.

But it wasn't as though Dunne had seen a trend others had missed, the hidden links between the world of dreams, arcane laws of physics, the unconscious and the intangible, tying them in ways that were comprehensible and elegant. The book relies too much upon complex looking yet vague maths for that. And it didn't matter that some of his mathematical assumptions had to be accepted otherwise they were hard to follow, just the possibility that time could be salvaged was enough. Freud and Einstein had triggered something not quite relevant to what they'd actually written, but people were hungry for arguments that challenged the grimly unswerving rules of nature, the same rules that had ordained death as inevitable.

All theories need a name and Dunne called his seriality. *It is still so new* (he wrote in *Nothing Dies*) *that you will not find the word in any English dictionary.* Or maybe lexicographers weren't ready to define something they couldn't understand. It relied on a series of selfs observing a previous one, which more or less did away with the need for past and future, since all observations occurred simultaneously, a bit like standing between two mirrors and seeing yourself from both sides infinitely regress. Even Jorge Luis Borges, who made a career teasing out obscure paradoxes, was hesitant to say what serialism was, but he was happy that it appeared we could select moments from our lives and reorganize them as we wanted, with Shakespeare (or any other historical figure) as our collaborator. Another way to put it: Death is not the end.

Meanwhile, there was a small army of thinkers, Helena Blavatsky, Aleister Crowley, Gurdjieff and Ouspensky, Bergson, various members of the Society for Psychical Research, René Guénon, not to mention returnees from Tibet and adherents of yoga who could be considered fellow travellers, so far as they weren't challenged by Dunne's ideas.

> Usually we think that the past already does not exist. It has passed, disappeared, altered, transformed itself into something else. The future also does not exist – it does not exist as yet. It has not arrived, has not formed.

That was Piotr Ouspensky, in his 1920 book *Tertium Organum*. He was never as popular as Dunne but his followers tended to come from science and medicine. Later he'd put it more simply. *It is possible that space and time are different aspects of the one reality,* which sounds just like the kind of idea that might have excited young John William Dunne when he was convalescing in Belgravia.

Meanwhile, *An Adventure* kept being reprinted, reviewed, and discussed, the only difference was that after Eleanor Jourdain's death there was no point hiding behind pseudonyms. The premise was addictive enough: the past was not past, it had moved to another plane, and every so often the membrane broke, allowing past, present or future to leach through. Cyril Joad, Britain's most popular radio philosopher, found the book too slippery for orthodox explanations, and he had bothered to head to Versailles with a copy of *An Adventure* and retrace the route the women had taken.

In 1931 Edith Olivier edited an edition. She had no doubt her two friends had experienced something. They had each staked their reputations on the story, and there were not only discrepancies between old and newer maps of the gardens that supported their descriptions. There were also rumours that others had seen odd things at Versailles. Edith Olivier described *An Adventure* as a *record of an unexplained extension of the limits of human experience.*

What she left out was her own experience of wild time. In 1916, she was stationed in Wiltshire with the local Women's Land Army. On an October evening, with a constant drizzle in the air, she drove up to the village of Avebury, famous for being located within a stone circle. Despite the rain, she wanted a view of the village in the stones, so she parked her car on a rise, near an avenue of megaliths and got out. Down below a fair was taking place.

> The grand megaliths and the humble cottages alike were partly obscured by the failing light and the falling rain, but both were fitfully lit by flares and torches from booths and shows. Some rather primitive swing-boats flew in and out of this dim circle of light; coconuts rolled hairily from the sticks on which they had been planted; bottles were shivered by gun-shots and tinkled as they fell to the ground.

Nine years later she returned to Avebury, and while telling someone about her experience was surprised to hear the last village fair had been in the 1850s.

But now there seemed to be no doubt that in October 1916 I had watched a scene which must have taken place at least sixty-six years earlier.

She made no mention of that experience until she wrote her autobiography, *Without Knowing Mr Walkley*, in 1938, but she did call on Dunne for a prefatory note to her edition of *An Adventure*, reasoning that he, if anyone, would have an explanation, and he did.

Marie Antoinette – body and brain – is sitting in the Trianon garden now. But what does that 'now' mean? Obviously, it cannot mean the three-dimensional 'now' of the ordinary, three-dimensional individual. It is a four-dimensional 'now', such as would be employed by a super-mind which could perceive Marie Antoinette and you (who are reading this) as equally present to perception.

Whether or not Charlotte Moberly and Eleanor Jourdain, and for that matter Edith Olivier, could be considered super-minds was a good question Dunne avoided. Not that it mattered. By the late 1930s his star was fading. Not surprising really; once the initial excitement had passed there remained the problem whether anything he claimed could be tested. But maybe that didn't matter either; Einstein had moved on and was discussing wormholes, which opened a whole new world of time travel, to a new generation who could imagine it well outside the confines of dreams. Even science fiction writers were creating invasions from the fourth dimension, *The Other Side of Here*, *The Man Who Went Back*, or they could turn to Charles Fort, who had spent years cutting anomalous stories from the newspapers and filing them into a database, warning his readers that his elaborate solutions to various mysteries were no more fatuous than the standard explanations.

On May 14, 1937, ninety-year-old Charlotte Moberly died. Later that year ghost hunter Harry Price received a manuscript from a stranger calling himself J. R Sturge-Whiting. *The Mystery of Versailles, a complete solution* might have been sent to Borley Rectory, where Price was staying at the time.

Price was determined to prove the rectory and its grounds was the most haunted building in England, literally crawling with ghostly monks and nuns. Later, eyewitnesses signed statements declaring he was determined enough to fake tests. Calling Price a ghost hunter or parapsychologist is inadequate. He was sceptical of mediums and exposed several as frauds, yet he insisted others were the real thing. A few years earlier he had scoffed at Gef the talking mongoose who lived on the Isle of Man, complaining that someone was after a quick buck, but you could say the same about his books like *Fifty Years of Psychical Research*, where he was careful to sound objective while feeding readers hints that there might after all be something to ghosts and haunted houses. A sceptic who loved the limelight, he was an obvious person to approach if you you'd written a book demythologizing a famous episode of time-travel and you needed a publisher.

John Ronald Sturge Whiting had served in the Navy during World War One, and not much more is, or was, known about him. The hyphen was never used in his military records. There's no evidence of formal education in science or history in *The Mystery of Versailles* but it has rigour. Sturge-Whiting went to

Versailles and followed the path outlined in the book, then he parsed each sentence as he traced the women's route according to their descriptions, reading contemporary plans against historical ones. This was a man who kept his desk spotless and his papers in order. He is curiously diplomatic.

*The story contains*, he said early on, *the ring of truth*, but the two women, he decided, had seen nothing out of the ordinary. When there could be a rational explanation they inevitably preferred the imaginative, so their 'mysterious cottage' was a common potting shed, and there was the problem of time, which had a way of emphasizing the oddness in peoples' dress (whatever that was) to the extent that much later it was easy to imagine it had been dress from another age. Sturge-Whiting could never be persuaded time travel was possible, but: *To these brave ladies The Adventure was vividly and patently true. If I find truth in its complete negation, then it is indeed the same truth, and honour is satisfied.*

At least he was willing to concede that they were not frauds. Some of their best friends weren't so generous.

As a young student, Joan Evans had suffered a series of never specified crises of confidence. Margaret Jourdain had stepped up and recommended she enrol at St Hugh's, where no one would laugh at her neuroses. Half a century later she was a respected art historian, author of books on medieval jewellery, biographies of French artists and politicians and histories of art in the Middle Ages. She was also the executrix of Charlotte Moberly and Eleanor Jourdain's estates, which effectively put all further editions of *An Adventure* in her hands.

Her introduction to the 1955 edition was important; she'd known both women well and could vouch for their characters, even though she warned in her introduction she wouldn't be flattering. That said, some of her assessments verged more on the side of pre-Darwin weird. Charlotte Moberly *had the narrow square head often found in the middle ranks of the Anglican clergy* and to be damning with faint praise, *her occasional flashes of insight and shrewdness were always astonishing.* Likewise, Eleanor Jourdain was *a woman of many talents rather than one dominating gift,* and, *her enthusiasms were rarely for people, and then for people she did not know...She would have wished to be a painter or a mystic philosopher: yet fate turned her first into a school-mistress and then into a woman don.*

So, a strange pair to begin with, but to her credit Evans defended them against the critics like Sturge-Whiting. She found sources that backed their accounts of buildings that were no longer there, but more importantly, she didn't dismiss the accounts. Charlotte Moberly and Eleanor Jourdain had experienced something, and it wasn't her place to tell them what that had been, just yet.

Twenty years later, in October 1976 Evans published an article in the British magazine *Encounter.* By now she could add a small list of fellowships and honorary doctorates to her achievements and she'd been awarded a Legion of Honour by France, so a powerful figure in the British establishment. Whatever respect she felt for her former teachers was waning. It was time to put an end to the stupid stories about Versailles, but there wasn't much to go on. The second-hand accounts in magazines knew better than to doubt the mystery. Good tabloid writers left the reader convinced something strange had happened. She needed to clear the air.

*An End to An Adventure: solving the mystery of the Petit Trianon* took a half-baked theory that had been floating about, disregarded its vagueness and put it at the centre of her solution.

At the end of the Nineteenth Century Robert de Montesquiou was a poet and painter though not much remembered for that now. According to the publisher Edmond de Goncourt he had real literary talent; he also owned a tortoise that he had professionally gilded then studded with gems so as it trundled about his apartment the lights bounced off the walls.

De Montesquiou was just as famous for his parties, attended by the fashionable elite like Sarah Bernhardt, Alphonse Daudet and Marcel Proust. They were not mere gatherings of people of course but elaborately staged events, and sometimes he threw them in the grounds at Versailles. So it made sense if on the afternoon of August 10, 1901, he had a party on the grounds and all his friends, the poets, the painters and the dilettantes had dressed as characters from the Ancien Regime and run through the gardens.

That was it, Joan Evans decided: mystery solved.

Except that one of Britain's pre-eminent art historians had failed to do her research. Like all social butterflies, de Montesquiou wanted people to know where he was and where he might be, just in case he missed that precious invite, and like all butterflies he flitted about, Paris in the spring and south to Nice for the summer, or Saint Malo or Sicily if friends were heading there. Also – and worse for Joan Evans – because he had such an intense grasp of his value to society he had a secretary, Antoine

Bertrand, taking care of his diaries. Bertrand noted parties not far from Versailles, a few years earlier, but never in the grounds on August 10, 1901.

It doesn't get better. Joan Evans was saying that two relatively sensible women weren't able to tell the difference between a masquerade and a group of phantoms when they encountered them. They could, most people can. If de Montesquiou and his friends were running about the woods in fancy dress that day and Charlotte Moberly and Eleanor Jourdain bumped into them, the two women would have returned to Oxford with a funny anecdote that lasted one telling.

But Evans shot her own theory down before she'd even got started. What the two women saw, she explained at the start, was a dress rehearsal for the party, which would account for it being left out of appointment books and the Palace's own records. Charlotte Moberly and Eleanor Jourdain, *might not have realized that 3:30 pm...is not a likely moment for a French fancy dress fete in August.*

Quite.

But Joan Evans wasn't finished. The flaws in her argument were obvious. Something had to explain why two relatively sensible women who were also honest would claim to have travelled through time to the last days of Marie Antoinette. When the facts won't stand up, theory will, and Evans turned to that popular and always ready source, Freud.

Trauma and repressed memories trigger unease, the inanimate takes on life, the familiar becomes strange: welcome to Freud's theory of the Uncanny. For Joan Evans sex was the problem. Not Charlotte Moberly and Eleanor Jourdain's so much as Robert de Montesquiou's. Especially the way he flaunted his preferences. The women they encountered that day weren't actually women but transvestites, and the gloom, the sense of foreboding the two scholars felt along the path wasn't that at all. *The ladies' sense of distaste and discomfort with all these people is a credit to their morals and their breeding.*

That was one way to take Freud's theory and run off with it. There was another.

When Lucille Parks arrived at St Hugh's in the 1930s, Charlotte Moberly had been retired for nearly twenty years and Eleanor Jourdain dead at least five. The Versailles mystery was now folklore, clouded by the Cecilia Ady scandal and Eleanor Jourdain's heart attack, but a true ghost story, good for winter nights around the teapot.

While at St Hugh's. she met and soon married Thomas Iremonger, an up-and-coming lawyer, destined to become tory MP for Ilford North for twenty years. The arrangement was perfect. He could make money without thinking about it and she wrote historical biographies and children's books and romances drawn from their life in the Caribbean and the South Pacific.

Everything she published was based on her life experiences, so even when she invented characters, the landscape they inhabited was faithful to memory. She knew how men in power thought and the secrets to a happy marriage, and, just like the pictures in tourist brochures, how colourful and happy the inhabitants of the tropics really were.

She'd heard things at St Hugh's. Neither Charlotte Moberly nor Eleanor Jourdain had married; everyone knew why. Still, the possibility that they had travelled back in time gave the college a kind of lustre. When it came to writing about what happened at Versailles, being an old St Hugh's girl practically made her an eyewitness, but if she wanted the book to sell she needed a solution. Something that was sensible but wouldn't crush illusions, something that would keep her readers turning the page.

Iremonger had to think back first to her time at St Hugh's in the 1930s, then back from there to the 1900s, so memories not of real time but of other memories. She recalled a saying around St Hugh's; "have you crossed Jordan yet?" Meaning, had Eleanor Jourdain made a pass at you? It wouldn't have been said when she was a student of course, maybe not even when Jourdain was alive, but it could have been one of those stories passed down into folklore, along with the cold, grey atmosphere of repressed Victorian affections. In this recasting of events, women forever dressed in widow black wandered the halls, the scratch of their footfalls against the timber floors accompanied by the flickering shadows cast by their candlelight. Part predator, part victim themselves, requests were never uttered but made clear with a raised eyebrow or the subtle brush of a hand against the skirt.

You could read Freud the way he wanted you to: repression of desire meant that desire manifested itself in other outlets. Or you could read him for the litany of odd sexual behaviours and practices that went on below the surface. To Iremonger it was apparent that because the attraction that Charlotte Moberly and Eleanor Jourdain had for each other, or for other women, could not be expressed openly, it went underground, coming up as one more wild exhibition of hysteria, the folie à deux, the shared hallucination.

Wandering through the gardens at Versailles, two women powerfully attracted to each other but without the permission to say so, found another way to share their lives, in a way every bit as personal as if they were holding hands. They began to imagine the gardens coming to life with the phantoms who really did haunt Versailles, everyone who came here sought some form of contact with them, but for once private bonds were so strong, they had the energy to bring spirit forces to life. Gardeners pushed barrows, messengers hurried to deliver fateful news, a woman sketched.

Psychiatrists recognize the folie à deux as a condition and can cite other examples, but were the phantoms pure figments or something else?

If this was a journey back in time then it appeared that the two women didn't simply go back to a particular instant, but several now re-enacted at once. Some years later Charlotte Moberly read Einstein and decided his theory did make her experience possible, but would even Einstein conceive of a multitude of temporal events all occurring simultaneously on the same plane? Another possibility was that time lengthened like a rubber band. All those events, the gardeners at work, the messengers running, the woman sketching, the hideous man by the kiosk, had happened, though not on the same day. Like an overstretched rubber band however, shape, or chronology, had been worn down. The ghostly participants were doomed to enact simple gestures; a messenger runs down a wooded path, Marie Antoinette holds a pencil over a sketchblock, about to begin a new drawing, over and over and over again until time forgets about them.

But time wasn't the only problem, and actually not the strangest. That network of students and teachers emerging from St Hugh's mattered, because it belonged to the schizoid world of women's colleges. Determined to advance the cause of women yet steadfast in their conservatism, they produced scholars expected to deliver original work while sitting comfortably within establishment diktats. Eleanor Jourdain organized rallies for women's suffrage and taught a generation of girls to believe philosophy mattered, all the time with a sick elephant in the room. Lucille Iremonger and Joan Evans could imagine radical solutions to the mystery because they believed the justifications were abhorrent. To Lucille Iremonger, both women, especially Eleanor Jourdain had secrets so dark her unconscious self couldn't hold them back. Joan Evans thought the problem wasn't with them so much as Robert de Montesquiou and his friends. Whichever way you looked at it, forbidden sex was where the rot began.

In 1955 the same year Joan Evans published the final authorized edition of *An Adventure*, Michele Basso died. Einstein's colleague, accomplice, sounding board and confidant, (though Einstein would say those adjectives didn't go halfway to describing the importance of their relationship) his significance to theoretical physics is rarely mentioned today. And maybe he'd be forgotten but in a letter to Basso's family reflecting on the passing of his friend, Einstein (who was close to death himself) wrote what would become one of his most enduring quotes about the nature of time: *People like us, who believe in physics, know that the distinction between past, present, and future is only a stubbornly persistent illusion.*

The people like us Einstein referred to was a small and exclusive club; he was on first name terms with every member. For them, belief in physics was more than an expression of faith; it required knowledge, which itself demanded sacrifice. To know that past, present and future are illusions was not some mystical invocation but a privilege for the people whose lives were devoted to understanding the mechanics of time.

Einstein was offering comfort to the family of his friend, but he was also expressing something of the exquisite pain that anyone who has been given a glimpse of the other side, the boundary region between life and death, the secret laws that govern our lives, the land over the ocean will always feel. We went there, Einstein told Basso's family. We saw it. He could have been talking about a strange land, with people and a culture just recognizable to his own, but different enough to fill him with wonder.

Eleanor Jourdain believed she had been there too, though Einstein knew they were talking about different places.

# SOURCES

## Introduction

The best account of the Yangchow headstones is by Francis Rouleau, *The Yangchow Latin Tombstone as a Landmark of Medieval Christianity in China* in "The Harvard Journal of Asiatic Studies", Vol. 17, Dec., 1954. "Discovery and Empire: The French and the South Seas", edited by John West Sooby, includes Margaret Sankey's The Abbé *Paulmier's Mémoires and Early French Voyages in Search of Terra Australis,* (University of Adelaide Press, 2013). Gabriel de Foigny's description of the South Land has the bombastic title, *A New Discovery of Terra Incognita Australis or the Southern World by James Sadeur a French-Man Who Being Cast There by a Shipwrack Lived 35 Years in That Country and Gives a Particular Description of the Manners Customs Religion Laws Studies and Wars of Those Southern People ; and of Some Animals Peculiar to That Place: With Several Other Rarities : These Memoirs Were Thought so Curious That They Were Kept Secret in the Closet of a Late Great Minister of State and Never Published Till Now Since His Death.* It was printed by John Dunton in 1693. Among the hundreds of books written about the North and South Poles, two referred to here are Donald Baxter MacMillan's account of the Crocker Land Expedition, Four Years in the White North (1918) and Valerian Al'banov's *In the Land of White Death, An Epic Story of Survival in the Siberian Arctic* (Modern Library 2001). There is also William Reed's 1906 book, *The Phantom of the Poles*, discussing the hollow Earth theory.

## Marguerite and the Isle of Demons

The earliest accounts of Marguerite de la Rocque appear in Marguerite de Navarre's *The Heptameron: Tales and Novels of Marguerite, Queen of Navarre*. The 1924 version was edited by Arthur Machen. *Andre Thevet's North America: A 16ᵗʰ Century World View*, edited by Roger Schlesinger and published by McGill Queen's University Press in 1986 contains the English version of Thevet's interview with Marguerite de la Rocque. Donald Johnson's *Phantom Islands of the Atlantic: The Legends of Seven Lands That Never Were*, published by Souvenir Press in 1997, includes a history of the floating locations of the Isle of Demons. The two relatively recent accounts of Marguerite's stay on the Isle of Demons are in Arthur Stabler's 1972 book *The Legend of Marguerite de Roberval* (Washington State University Press) and Elizabeth Boyer's *A Colony of One: The History of a Brave Woman*, published by Veritie Press in 1983.

## The Long Forgotten Walk of David Ingram

David Ingram's account appears in *Documents Connected with the History of South Carolina*, published in 1856. Extracts and statements confirming Ingram's story are in *The Voyages of the English Nation to America*, Vol 2, Richard Hakluyt, 1889, and *Divers Voyages Touching upon the Discoverie of America, printed by* Thomas Woodcocke in 1582) George Peckham, A True

Report of the late Discovery and Possession, taken in the Right of the Crowne of Englande, of the Newfound Landes. The meeting with John Dee is in *The Private Diary of Dr. John Dee, edited by* James O. Halliwell in 1842. John Aubrey's, *Brief Lives,* edited Oliver Dick, (Penguin, 1972) contains Aubrey's comments on Dee. Hakluyt's *Voyages of the English Nation* opens with a chapter on Madoc. Alvar Nunez Cabeza de Vaca's *Chronicle of the Narvaez Expedition* was published by Penguin in 2002. *An Account of several late voyages & discoveries to the south and north...By Sir John Narborough, Captain Jasmen Tasman, Captain John Wood, and Frederick Marten,* to give it a workable title, was published in 1724.

## The Lost Dutchman

The Batavia journal of Francisco Pelsaert was edited and translated by Marit van Huystee for the Dept. of Maritime Archaeology, Western Australian Maritime Museum in 1998. It is the only authentic translation into English of the full journal although John Pinkerton referred to it in *Early Australian Voyages: Pelsart Tasman Dampier,* published by Cassell in 1893. Mike Dash's *Batavia's Graveyard,* published by Weidenfeld & Nicolson in 2002 is the most thorough account of what happened at the Archipelago. J. E Heeres described Dutch voyages to the Australian coast in *The Part Borne by the Dutch in the Discovery of Australia 1606-1765 (1899)* and edited *Abel Janszoon Tasman's Journal* in 1898. R H Major's *Early Voyages to Terra Australis, now called Australia,* (1963) accounts for most of the Dutch expeditions of the seventeenth century. Miriam

Estensen's *Discovery: the Quest for the Great South Land* (Palgrave, 1999) updates a lot of the information. *Mary Ann Friend's journal of a voyage to Hobart with account of the settlement on the Swan River, 1829-1831*, is in the rare books section of the State Library of Western Australia; a transcript is online. George Fletcher Moore's *Diary of ten years eventful life of an early settler in Western Australia; and also, A descriptive vocabulary of the language of the Aborigines* was published by the University of Western Australia Press in 1978. Rupert *Gerritsen's And Their Ghosts May Be Heard* (1994) argued that the Dutch had landed on Western Australian coast and bred with local Aboriginal women. The English translation of Jean-Pierre Purry's work on climate was published in 1744 as *A method for determining the best climate of the earth : on a principle to which all geographers and historians have been hitherto strangers, in a memorial presented to the Governors of the East-India Company in Holland, for which the author was obliged to leave that country, by* John Peter Purry.

## A Time in Versailles

*An Adventure* has been in print since 1911, but only the 1911, the 1913, the 1924, the 1931 and 1955 editions matter. There are changes in each, with chapters moved around, commentaries added in some then removed in later versions but the accounts of Moberly and Jourdain's walk through the gardens of the Petit Trianon remain the same. The first two editions Moberly and Jourdain published under their pseudonyms, Elizabeth Morison and Frances Lamont. The 1931 edition was edited by Edith Olivier, the 1955 edition was edited by Joan Evans. J. W.

Dunne's *An Experiment with Time* also went through numerous editions. For this, the 1939 edition published by Faber and Faber was used. Lucille Iremonger's *The Ghosts of Versailles: Miss Moberly and Miss Jourdain and their adventure: a critical study*, was published by White Lion in 1975. Eleanor Jourdain's *On the Theory of the Infinite in Modern Thought* was published by Longmans in 1911. Edith Olivier's account of her own time slip appeared in *Without Knowing Mr. Walkley: Personal Memories,* published by Readers' Union in 1938. Her description of Charlotte Moberly appeared in *Four Victorian Ladies of Wiltshire,* Faber and Faber, 1945. J. R Sturge-Whiting's *The Mystery of Versailles, a complete solution* appeared in 1938.

John Toohey is a writer and photographer who lives in Canada. He has published many books and has written articles for *The Conversation* (Canada), *Public Domain Review* (US), *The Pomegranate* (UK) and academic journals such as *Early Popular Visual Culture*. He has post-graduate degrees in photography and history. His photographs are held in major collections.